D1523545

Hard Knocks

PREPARING YOUTH FOR WORK

Bonnie Snedeker

Foreword by Sar A. Levitan

THE JOHNS HOPKINS UNIVERSITY PRESS
Baltimore and London

All names of persons interviewed in this book are fictitious. Any coincidence of these names with those of real people is unintentional. The photographs are not of the persons interviewed.

Photographs on pages xii, 96, and 112 are by the Division of Occupational Outlook, Bureau of Labor Statistics, U.S. Department of Labor. Photographs on pages 18, 48, 76, and 146 are by Ed Kashi.

The Johns Hopkins University Press, Baltimore, Maryland 21218
The Johns Hopkins Press Ltd., London

Library of Congress Cataloging in Publication Data

Snedeker, Bonnie B.
    Hard knocks.

    Bibliography: p. 169
    Includes index.
    1. Youth—United States—Interviews. 2. Poor—United States—Interviews. 3. Youth—Employment—United States—Interviews. 4. Socially handicapped youth—United States—Interviews. I. Title.
HQ796.S554   305.2'35'0973   82-7751
ISBN 0-8018-2823-6   AACR2

Contents

Foreword

Hundreds of millions of dollars have been spent on research and demonstration activities aimed at determining the causes, consequences, and cures for "youth problems." Libraries are filled with empirical studies of family environment, educational achievement, and the transition of youth from school to work. There are ample statistics to prove a researcher's biases and to dress them up as objective analyses. Even in this conservative era, the output of youth reports continues; yet answers and solutions remain elusive.

The basic reason is that the experiences of youth are dynamic, complex, and diverse. They are not easily captured by statistics or enlightened by mathematical models. Sophisticated and efficient as today's data-gathering and analysis techniques may be, computers have yet to master a methodology for regressing the full impact of a broken home, an unemployed parent, academic failure, or out-of-wedlock childbearing upon the life of a teen-ager. To gain insights into the problems faced by youth, it is necessary to probe their family backgrounds, their attitudes, their perceptions of themselves and their environments. The best way to do this is through first-hand observations and interactions.

Hard Knocks offers a refreshing description of the ways young people aged seventeen to twenty cope with multiple problems. Bonnie Snedeker interviewed several hundred low-income participants in federally supported employment and training programs. She selected sixteen youths, equally divided between blacks and whites, living in Boston, Massachusetts, Kalamazoo, Michigan, and Portland, Oregon. These young people speak for themselves and thousands like them who live in the low-income neighborhoods, ghettos, and housing projects of our cities. Snedeker taped these conversations, and she presents the views of the youngsters forcefully and with a minimum of editorializing.

Several observations emerge from the compelling stories of these young people. First, enormous diversity is revealed in these individual profiles. There are dramatic differences in circumstance, perspective, ability, and potential. This vivid reminder of the infinite range of human variation makes the criteria by which youth are generally categorized seem woefully inadequate. Clearly, any conclusions about cause-and-effect relationships or program impacts that depend on quantifiable characteristics cannot explain the realities of individual cases. This requires going beyond objective measures, averages, and trends.

Second, it is apparent that these young people are not outside the mainstream by choice. They are marked by their past failures and difficulties, but their aspirations and hopes for the future tend to be, if anything, rather more conventional than those of more advantaged youth. They have experienced life on the streets, in correctional facilities, and in broken homes, and most of them want stable homes, families, and jobs. They are willing to work but lack adequate employment preparation, information, or opportunities.

Third, the young people turn to employment and training programs because other avenues are blocked. Earlier failures at home, at school, and in the community effectively cut them off from most of the usual routes of transition to the working world. But by the time they are entering their late teens, the barriers to their employability are apt to be substantial. The young women who turn to welfare to support their out-of-wedlock children may find it nearly impossible to break out of poverty. While some of the youths are able to take advantage of the opportunities provided by the programs and move into entry-level employment after a minimum investment of time and resources, others with more severe problems find that the programs offer limited possibilities for dealing with the full range of their needs.

Fourth, the stories of the sixteen young people clearly portray the breakdown of the institutions that traditionally have supported the rearing and development of children. The interventions established by the welfare state have helped many, but more are left inadequately protected. The current retrenchments in the alternative mechanisms developed over the past two decades will result in the neglect of many more young adults.

Hard Knocks does not provide scientific measures or policy prescriptions, yet its sympathetic and probing discussions with youth in need yield more insights than volumes of technical studies. This study furthers the understanding of youth problems that cannot be obtained by poring over computerized data untouched by human hands or hearts.

Sar A. Levitan

Acknowledgments

The debts I have accumulated in researching and writing this book are so numerous and substantial that any form of acknowledgment seems inadequate. Most profoundly, I am grateful to the young people who participated in the interviews and were willing to share their experiences, feelings, and ideas. This book is really theirs, and I regret that the requirements of confidentiality do not allow me to acknowledge them by name. Also indispensable were the youth program counselors and supervisors in Boston, Portland, and Kalamazoo who helped set up interviews and contributed their own observations and insights to the research.

The process of conceptualizing and designing the research for this book began more than five years ago. David Snedeker and Garth Mangum were important influences in the development of the ideas behind the research. I thank Bob Taggart for encouraging me to move from concept to action. The research was supported in part by a grant from the U.S. Department of Labor, under the direction of the National Council on Employment Policy. Greg Wurzburg, former executive director of the council, provided substantial support and assistance. Seymour Brandwein, from the Office of Program Evaluation, U.S. Department of Labor, was also pivotal in the development of the project.

I am indebted to David Stallings, from Osoro and Associates, whose enthusiasm and advice were important factors in translating the interview material into manuscript form. I would like to thank the following people who reviewed the manuscript in its various stages: R. C. Smith, Marion Pines, Rupert Evans, Vernon Briggs, Mary Conway Kohler, Patricia Auspos, Jim Fraser, June Cid, and Katherine Hughes. Their suggestions were of great value. Credit is due to Ed Kashi, who is responsible for the cover design and most of the photographs in the book. The photographs facing chapters one, five, and six were provided by the Division of Occupational Outlook, U.S. Bureau of Labor Statistics. I am grateful to Penny Blankenship, whose involvement in this project began with the transcribing of the interview tapes and continued through the skillful typing and proofreading of the final manuscript.

Finally, I owe a special debt to my family and friends, who learned to live with my preoccupation and who weathered my periods of obsession with grace and understanding.

Hard Knocks

1. Who Are We?

The Lives behind the Statistics

> Before I came here, I wasn't doin' nothin'. Stayin' out on the street, you know? Comin' in late every night, wakin' up late every mornin'. I wasn't really innerested in nothin'. I stealed weed. Rode around in stolen cars. Gettin' money never really phased me—I could always get money from people I knew. You know, doin' certain things, you can always get money. But I got to thinkin'—it was about time for me to get movin'—get *in* something—either full-time workin' or goin' to school. I knew sooner or later I'd haffta do *something*—you know, I never really saw myself bein' one of those dudes just hangin' out.   *Bobby Jones*

Eighteen-year-old Bobby Jones lives in a public-housing project in Boston. When he showed up at a community center near his home to apply for work with a federally funded youth employment and training project, Bobby had been out of school and out of work for nearly two years. He spent his time watching television, shooting baskets in the community gym, and hanging around the housing project, getting into trouble. Bobby says that he always intended to work, but he never spent much time looking for a job. Apart from the street hustlers around the project, he did not know anyone who had much use for a black teen-ager who had left school in the ninth grade.

Sandy Bonds was fourteen when she first left her mother's home in Maryland. She hitched a ride to Phoenix, where she planned to live with her father and finish high school. When things did not work out there, she moved on to Albuquerque. By the time she decided to settle down in Oregon, Sandy had lived in five different states in four years. She was eighteen when she came to a city-operated youth center in Portland looking for help to find a job. Sandy had been out of school for more than two years, but she did not know much about the world of work:

> I've traveled all around, but I haven't worked much, you know? 'Cause most the time, I was livin' with a foster parent or with friends, and they were always tryin' to get me back in school. The only job I can really say I ever had was bein' like a housekeeper

·1·

for five months for this one family in Washington. And I worked at Burgerville once for about two days. I always had it in mind to work, but I didn't have any skills—didn't know what I wanted to work *as,* you know? I learned how to get by out on the street. But *working*—I just plain don't know very much about it. I don't know what I could do with myself once I had the skills.

Carmeletta DeVries has lived all of her seventeen years in a predominantly black neighborhood in Kalamazoo, Michigan. For most of her life, Carmeletta lived with her mother. She went to the public high school near her home until she became pregnant during the tenth grade. Carmeletta decided to drop out of school, keep her baby, and raise him on her own. She applied for welfare and left her mother's house to move into an apartment with her older sister. When her son was nine months old, Carmeletta started looking for a job. She was tired of staying home with the baby, and she felt that her life was going nowhere:

> I sit home with my baby every day, and I don't like it really—I don't. If my boyfriend don't come around, I never have nobody to be with. I don't never *go* nowhere. I been lookin' for a job—it's hard to find. Since my son was born, I been livin' with my sister and her two kids. I get some welfare, you know, but it's no good. My mother always told me I should finish school. Back when she was young, you could get a job easy. But now it's gettin' to where you need something—some education, experience, first—before you can get a job. I wish I could go back—I'd be graduatin' this year if I'd stayed and stuck to it, you know, if I didn't have a baby. But havin' a baby—it's a change, you know? It really is.
>
> Myself, I can feel that I'm gettin' older. You know, I'm out here on my own and everything, tryin' to make it the best way I can. I just wanna get me a good job. Then I wanna get me a deposit for an apartment. And I don't want it to be too much longer.

What happens to young people like Bobby, Sandy, and Carmeletta? They are on their own and need money to support themselves. They want to work but do not know how to get started in the working world. They have no experience and no marketable skills. They have left school without the diploma that most employers associate with base-level competency. They have no institutional ties and no informal relationships they can lean on for support in making the transition to an adult working life. Out of school and out of work, they live outside the mainstream of American life. Unlike most middle-class teen-agers, whose childhoods are prolonged through extended involvement in school and family life, they have not been sheltered from adult realities. The circumstances of their lives demand self-reliance beyond that normally required of people their age. But the survival skills they have developed to face life on the streets, in the ghetto, or on the margins of society are not likely to be viewed as assets by the guardians of the work place.

In the fall of 1978 Bobby, Sandy, and Carmeletta enrolled in employment and training programs that were funded by the federal government and designed to provide immediate work and income while improving the long-range employment prospects of economically disadvantaged youth. Programs of this kind were initiated during the 1960s as the first wave of youth from the postwar baby boom was entering the labor force. The programs were expanded in the 1970s as the population of fourteen- to twenty-one-year-olds grew and youth unemployment skyrocketed. The programs for which Bobby, Sandy, and Carmeletta signed up were authorized under the Youth Employment and Demonstration Projects Act of 1977 (YEDPA), which provided a substantial but temporary boost in the program resources earmarked for youth under the preexisting authorization of the Comprehensive Employment and Training Act (CETA). During fiscal years 1978 through 1980 an extensive array of new CETA jobs and employment preparation services was provided to eligible young people by state and local government agencies, school systems, and nonprofit community organizations. This expansion of CETA youth programs under YEDPA reflected the culmination of concern felt by Congress and the Carter administration toward the problems of youth unemployment. Though the problems have not abated, national priorities have shifted during the early years of the Reagan administration. In 1981 CETA youth programs were cut back to pre-YEDPA levels. The outlook for continued funding is uncertain.

I met Bobby, Sandy, and Carmeletta during the initial stages of a year-long research project. They were among several hundred young people that I interviewed from CETA programs in Boston, Kalamazoo, and Portland. My interviews were designed to capture information on the life styles, values, employment preparation, and labor-market experiences of young people who experience extended periods of joblessness and who face substantial barriers in making a successful transition to the world of work. I was interested in looking behind the statistics on youth poverty, unemployment, and participation in government programs.

I had been involved for several years in research on CETA youth programs. Along with other researchers across the country, I examined national and local indicators of employment problems and training needs in the youth population, traced the development of service-delivery systems, and analyzed data on program enrollments, costs, completion rates, and job placement results. Our studies, commissioned by the federal government, provided insights on how national policies are translated into programs and services in local communities. The reports we wrote described how youth employment and training programs were designed and conducted, who among the vast youth population was enrolled, and what immediate effects participation in programs seemed to have on the employment status of young people. Our reports described the programs, but they did not reveal much about the people these programs were designed to serve. They documented the characteristics of the participant population, but they did not help policy makers, program planners, administrators, trainers, or guidance counselors understand what it is like to be young, unemployed, and outside the mainstream of American life.

Teen-agers who are cut off from mainstream institutions—family, school, or work—are a primary target group for unemployment and training programs. But these "high-risk" teen-agers comprise only a minority of the applicants for youth programs, and the employment outcomes of those who do enroll in the programs are often disappointing. Youth program agencies charged with providing employment and training are often baffled in their attempts to serve teen-agers from the high-risk group. The CETA administrators, counselors, and work supervisors I interviewed were inclined to see these young people as undependable, unrealistic, and lacking in motivation and self-discipline. One counselor at a training site in Boston expressed a sense of frustration shared by many others when he told me: "These kids have experienced failure in every phase of their lives—at home, at school, and out in the community—and it shows on them. They're not ready to go to work. What can we do in six months' or even a year's time that will turn all that around?

That the problems these young people face are complex, are linked to failures in our social institutions, and are difficult to resolve in the context of limited employment and training resources is widely acknowledged. There is a massive archive of research on the causes and consequences of family breakdown, inadequate schooling, dysfunctional community life, and the inequitable distribution of income and employment opportunity. But I wanted to look more closely at the lives behind the statistics. How do young people like Bobby, Sandy, and Carmeletta see themselves and the problems they face? What do they have to say about their experiences at home, at school, and in their communities? How does participation in employment and training programs affect their lives? Where do they go when they leave the programs?

The young people whose stories are included in this book constitute only a small group among the thousands of high-risk teen-agers who live in our cities and shoulder a disproportionate burden of the employment problems in our country. I have chosen sixteen from among the several hundred young people whom I interviewed, and from the forty I followed more intensively during my year of research. Bobby, Sandy, Carmeletta, and the others in this group are real people—not composites. They willingly shared their experiences and insights as well as their expectations, hopes, and fears. To protect their privacy I have changed their names and those of their relatives, friends, and counselors. I have also made some changes in the names of housing projects, business establishments, and program agencies, as well as altered dates, attributes, or circumstances that might otherwise serve to reveal identities. My interviews with these young people were taped, and the words attributed to them have been taken from edited transcripts. I have tried not to tamper with the substance of their ideas and experiences. My goal has been to present, as clearly as I am able, the realities of their lives as they perceive them.

To digest and organize the experiences, feelings, and ideas of sixteen individuals is not easy. As I got to know Bobby, Sandy, Carmeletta, and the others, and as I reviewed the material I had collected from our interviews, I came to see them more clearly—both as distinct individuals and as reliable spokespersons for other young people who shared some of the same characteristics, problems, and aspirations. As I began the interviews I had only a limited frame of reference and little insight into the lives of these young people and the realities of their circumstances. The early stages of the research were both stimulating and confusing. I was meeting many new people, in settings I had not previously encountered. To introduce our group of young people, I would like to go back to my first visits to Boston, Kalamazoo, and Portland—to the community agencies, schools, and youth program centers where we first met.

Boston

My first interviews in Boston were scheduled with participants in a CETA weatherization project. The two-month-old project was providing full-time work at the minimum wage for eighteen young people, ranging in age from sixteen to nineteen, who were out of school and unemployed. The young people were given instruction by project staff and then sent out in supervised work crews to install weather stripping, vapor barriers, and other energy-saving devices in the homes of low-income people. The community center where project participants met each morning was located in Victoria Point, a public housing complex, which was not linked to central Boston by direct bus or subway service. The initial arrangements for my interviews had been made by people from the CETA youth program administrative office in Boston, who told me that the quickest and safest way to reach Victoria Point was by taxi.

An early morning taxi ride to Dorchester, in drizzling rain and rush-hour traffic, gave me ample time to worry about the interviews ahead. I had been warned that Victoria Point could be an inhospitable, and even dangerous, place for outsiders. Why should the black teen-agers who lived and worked there want to talk about their experiences with a white, and obviously middle-class, researcher from the Pacific Northwest? They would probably take me for some kind of social worker—one who had a funny accent and asked a lot of questions, but who came equipped with a pre-dictable set of preconceptions. I would be greeted either with amusement, as a potential source of diversion, or—more likely—with undisguised hostility.

As my thoughts ran on in this unpleasant way, I noticed that we had emerged from streets bordered by storefronts, aging clapboard houses, and trash-littered yards, and were traveling on an open highway that stretched along a promontory above Boston Harbor. We passed a deserted shopping mall, its windows boarded, and empty parking lots surrounded by fields of tall brown grass. Just beyond it on the headlands, I saw a complex of two- and four-story buildings and realized that we had reached Victoria Point. The car pulled over to a taxi stand near what appeared to be the main entrance to the housing project. My driver, who was white, announced that this was as far as he was going: "I got caught in here one night, just trying to do someone a favor, and I don't drive around in here no more." I got out of the car, trying to look more confident and nonchalant than I felt.

As I walked into the housing project to look for the community center, my trepidation grew. It was nine o'clock in the morning and the few people who were about were probably on their way to work and in a hurry. I hesitated to ask anyone for directions, and approached the nearest building as though I knew were I was going. It did not look promising: The vestibule was blackened by fire, broken glass and garbage covered a good part of the floor, and the graffiti sprayed across the charred walls seemed to be addressed directly to me. I quickly retreated down the front stairs and stepped out into the courtyard to look around. I realized then that the housing project was at least half-vacant. Most of the windows in the taller buildings were boarded up, and only the two-story buildings seemed to be inhabited. A young woman with a small child in tow was hurrying across the courtyard, and I asked her if she could tell me how to get to the community center. Her directions were simple; it was only a short walk to the two-story building, which was adorned by a multicolor mural and bright blue doors.

After receiving a greeting and a cup of coffee from a woman at the reception desk, my uneasiness dissipated, and I felt foolish over my exaggerated apprehension. The weatherization project director, I was told, knew of my visit but was unable to be at the center that day. Though I was to speak with him by telephone several times in the months that followed, the director was never in the building when I made my periodic visits, and we never spoke face to face. The work crew supervisors had been told I was coming, though they were not sure what I planned to do. They listened to my explanation with polite attention. They provided what seemed to be a standard description of a weatherization project and then talked more animatedly about their own roles in the project. While I was talking with the others, one of the supervisors went downstairs to solicit volunteers for the interviews.

None of the work crews was out that morning. The young people were in the center being taught how to measure materials. Most of them were eager to be interviewed. I met with each volunteer individually. I explained to them that I was a researcher, interviewing young people from different parts of the country, that I did not work for the city or for the community center. I was interested in how young people find out about the world of work and how employment and training programs work from their point of view. I told them I was looking for people who were willing to share their experiences and feelings about different parts of their lives, and I explained that participation in the interviews would be voluntary, unpaid, and would not effect their standing in the project.

For the most part, they accepted my interest in them as a matter of course and did not seem to doubt that their personal experiences and concerns were important in a broader context and were worthy of study. I was surprised at how responsive these teen-agers were and how easily and vividly they talked about their lives. I wanted to learn more about each of them, but three of the young people working on the weatherization project stood out most clearly.

Harold Thomas looked older than seventeen. He is a tall, muscular young man with a gentle manner and a faraway look in his eyes. When Harold first spoke, I noticed he had a Virginia drawl. He told me that he, his brother, and two younger sisters had moved from their hometown on the Eastern Shore of the Chesapeake Bay to live with an older sister in Boston, following the death of their parents in an automobile accident. That was more than two years ago, and Harold said he still had not adjusted to the change. He did not like Boston, and he did not think he ever would. Harold said he had dropped out of school in his junior year and had spent several months in the army reserves. He had been working on the weatherization project for only two weeks.

Genetta Burke was the only young woman in the weatherization project. At nineteen, she had the appearance and self-confidence of an attractive woman in her prime. She was dressed in a pantsuit, with a scarf around her neck, and she explained to me that she wore her street clothes to the center and only put on overalls when she was out on a job. Genetta is a welfare mother. She told me that she grew up in Victoria Point, but now lived a mile or so from the housing project in an apartment with her two children and elderly grandmother. She was among the first to sign up for the weatherization project and had been working there for about seven weeks. Genetta said the project was "okay," but she felt that she was more grown up than the young men on her crew:

> You know, the guys here, they're all like eighteen, nineteen years old, and they play like kids. They be thinkin' sometime that I think I'm better than them—just 'cause I don't like to joke or play around all the time. But I'm too old for that stuff, you know? It would be better with older, more mature people. You know, men are just babies until they're thirty!

Adam Sledge is a handsome young man, with dark skin, large eyes, and wavy hair. Though he seemed eager to appear grown up and was careful to maintain a knowing posture, there was an air of youthful inno- cence about him. Adam was eighteen and lived with his mother and six of his eight brothers and sisters in the Victoria Point housing project. Adam said he had recently dropped out of school, just after beginning the eleventh grade. His girlfriend was pregnant. As a prospective father, Adam felt he should be "out in the world workin' instead of sittin' in school like a child." He had been enrolled in the weatherization project for only one week and also had a part-time CETA job as a night security aide at Victoria Point.

The community center I visited the next day was in Dorchester, several miles from Victoria Point. This center served the residents of the smaller homes and private apartment complexes in the neighborhood, as well as people from the adjoining public-housing project. The building, though aging, was large and well maintained. It contained a full gymnasium, used for community recreation programs; a daycare center, used by the Head Start Program; and a large kitchen and cafeteria, used to provide noon meals for senior citizens. It also housed a CETA youth project that provided remedial education and part-time work for teen-agers.

Bobby Jones was the first young person that I interviewed at the community center. He is tall, black, and lean, and walks with athletic grace and a bit of a swagger. The CETA project director, John Henry, warned me that Bobby was "kind of a big talker," but I found him interesting and easy to listen to. Bobby told me that he lived with his older sister and two younger sisters, but did not spend much time at home. His mother died when he was in the seventh grade, and Bobby said that was when he started "havin' problems around bein' in school." After dropping out of school in the ninth grade, he spent two years on the streets. He had been involved in a number of illegal activities and had a juvenile offense record before he signed up for the CETA project. Bobby was eager to be included in the interviews, but he was dubious about my methods:

> Tape recordin' and writin' it down off the tapes ain't too sure a thing. You might get this *wrong*, you know? And if you make a book out of it, not too many people will read it anyway. Next time you come down here, why don't you bring a TV camera? You know, I want people·to see how it *really* is.

Luanne Clawson, who was enrolled in the CETA project with Bobby, is a frail-looking young woman with clear, honey-colored skin. She has a malformed palate, which causes her to speak with a slight lisp. Luanne said that she lived with her mother and younger sister in the housing project near the community center. When she first heard about the CETA project, Luanne was in the eleventh grade and struggling to keep up with her classmates at West Roxbury High School. She thought she might do better in the special classes at the community center, so she dropped out of school and signed up for the CETA project. She had been enrolled for only two weeks.

Most of the young people who enroll in Boston's youth employment programs are black. *Sven Latoka* was one of the few white teen-agers that I interviewed. We met at a community service agency housed in an old church in Jamaica Plain, a predominantly white, working-class section of Boston. Sven had just enrolled in a CETA renovation and construction project. He was nineteen; a strong, rawboned young man with a military haircut and the deferential manners of a marine recruit. After leaving school in the tenth grade, Sven had worked with his father and on his own and had spent time in the marine reserves. He wanted to be a carpenter, and he told me that he had signed up for the project because he was tired of "low-paying, dead-end jobs" and wanted steady work and employment references that would improve his prospects in his chosen field.

Felisa Santana was a student in a bilingual alternative school, operated by a Hispanic community agency in Boston. The school, where we met for our first interview, was located on the third and fourth floors of a narrow brick building in a Hispanic/Lebanese neighborhood. With her streaked hair, carefully applied make-up, and city clothes, Felisa looked more like a young working woman than a seventeen-year-old schoolgirl. She lived with her parents, who were unemployed, and five younger brothers and sisters. Although she was born in Puerto Rico, Felisa said she had spent most of her life in Boston. She attended public school in Boston from kindergarten until eighth grade. When Felisa was fourteen the Santanas returned to Puerto Rico. They spent two years there and then came back to Boston in 1977. Felisa did not want to return to public school—she was afraid that she would be bused out of her neighborhood. She spent six months at home before enrolling in a General Equivalency Diploma (GED) program at the bilingual school. The school was supported partially by CETA funds, and Felisa's counselor had helped her to get a part-time CETA job. She had been working and attending classes for seven months.

Kalamazoo

Kalamazoo County is in western Michigan. Nearly half the county's 200,000 people live in or near the City of Kalamazoo, an established manu-facturing and marketing center with busy shopping districts, a university and several colleges, and many striking and well-preserved Victorian homes. The city is surrounded by flat expanses of Michigan farmland, dotted with smaller communities such as Cooper, Galesburg, Oshtemo, and School-craft. I had visited Kalamazoo previously, because it had served as a research site for a study of youth program systems on which I had worked. I knew something about how youth program services were structured there, and I viewed Kalamazoo as a good example of a moderately pro-gressive, medium-sized Midwestern community.

Youth employment and training programs in Kalamazoo County are operated on a comprehensive basis by a special division of the Kalamazoo Valley Intermediate School District. Services are provided to eligible young people—both in school and out of school—through a facility located in the central downtown area. While the youth program agency serves young people in the outlying rural communities, as well as those in the city, the majority of teen-agers who are both out of school and out of work are clustered near the urban center. Most of the interviews I conducted in Kalamazoo were held at the youth program agency.

Carmeletta DeVries, the young welfare mother who was tired of "sitting home" alone every day, came to the youth program agency in Kalamazoo because she was unable to find a job on her own. Carmeletta's hair was braided in elaborate corn rows. She spoke very slowly, in a deep melodious voice. Although she seemed to be naturally reserved, she could also be candid and direct. "I love my son," she told me, "but I sure didn't *need* no baby. I never liked school when I was there. But now I wish I'd of stuck with it and not gotten pregnant, you know?" Carmeletta had recently been assigned to a full-time job through the CETA program, and she said she was having a hard time working and taking care of her baby.

Jack Thrush is a slightly built, quick-moving young man, with shoulder-length blond hair and a vigilant expression. Jack's counselor at the youth program agency warned me when we were setting up the interview that Jack seemed to have a difficult time keeping appointments. He showed up nearly two hours late—just as I was getting ready to leave. Jack was wary during our first interview, but he told me quite a bit about himself. He was eight years old when his father died, and he had lived with his mother and older brother until his brother left home to join the army and his mother remarried. When Jack was sixteen he dropped out of school, found a job as a busboy, and moved out of his mother's house to live with friends. He was seventeen and had been unemployed for about three months when he came to the youth program agency looking for work.

At first glance, *Carrie Green* looked like a Norman Rockwell cheerleader. She has long blond hair and a lanky, girlish figure. But her walk was listless and her pretty face devoid of expression. She thought for a long time before she spoke, in a flat Midwestern voice. After her parents divorced, when Carrie was ten, her family consisted of her father and two older sisters. Carrie said she left school in her sophomore year, at age fifteen, so that she could get a job and move out on her own. During the next two years she held a number of short-term, low-paying jobs, and she moved in and out of her father's house as her employment status fluctuated. She had been unemployed for two months when she came to the youth program agency in Kalamazoo.

Portland

Situated at the confluence of the Willamette and Columbia rivers in northwestern Oregon, Portland is a particularly attractive, well-kept city. With a population of about 390,000, it is Oregon's largest city, just over half the size of Boston and with three times the population of Kalamazoo. Though not seriously affected by physical decay or economic stagnation, Portland is not immune to the problems of crime, race discrimination, and high youth unemployment that plague older and larger cities. In the mid-1970s, Portland developed what many viewed as a model youth employment and training system. The city had frequently been used as a research site for studies on youth programs. I had worked in Portland on a number of occasions and was familiar with the system.

The City of Portland encompasses a wide geographic area with many different types of neighborhood. Access to youth employment and training services is coordinated through a comprehensive system, operated by the city, which maintains a youth service center in each quadrant of Portland. Most of Portland's black population is concentrated in the northeast quadrant. Most of the young people I interviewed came from the Southeast youth center, which served an industrial area inhabited largely by white, working-class people.

Sandy Bonds, who had been on the road for the better part of four years, said she had only been in Portland for about two weeks when she came to the Southeast center looking for work. Sandy is a petite young woman with bright blue eyes, a cloud of fair hair, and a fiercely independent, outspoken personality. Sandy was wearing heavy boots and baggy workclothes, and she told me that she was on her lunchbreak from her CETA job as a construction trainee. Sandy said she had been in and out of school for several years until she "quit for good" at age sixteen. She had a juvenile offense record in three different states for vagrancy, drug-dealing, truancy, and disorderly conduct. She was now eighteen and her CETA job was the first steady work she had had.

Douglas Giscard was also a client of the Southeast center. But we met for our first interview at the Street Shelter, a social service agency for runaways and other teen-agers out on their own, where Douglas had a CETA job as a staff aide. Douglas was an articulate, obviously intelligent eighteen-year-old. He is small and well built, with light-brown skin and long, jet-black hair. He told me his grandmother was an Indian and his father a French Canadian. He grew up in a middle-income family but left home when he was sixteen because he could not get along with his parents, who were strict disciplinarians. He dropped out of school in the tenth grade soon after leaving home. Douglas said he had been referred to the CETA program by his juvenile probation officer, following his arrest and conviction on burglary charges. He had been in the program for one month.

Tien Van Chin was seventeen—an alert, intense young man, with a pale, broad face and a nervous smile. Though he still had problems with English, he spoke rapidly and had an obvious fondness for American slang. Tien came from a once prosperous Chinese family in Saigon. He told me he had immigrated from Vietnam on his own before his fourteenth birthday. He came to Portland after spending nearly two years in a refugee camp in Thailand. Before he came to the Southeast center, Tien had worked in a number of different short-term, low-paying jobs. He had been enrolled in the CETA program for one month.

Jean Ansel is a slender but strong-looking young woman. She has straight, light-brown hair and wears no makeup. Her counselor at the Southeast center told me that Jean had been through a lot in her seventeen years—including a stint as a teen-age prostitute. I found Jean's skeptical and penetrating gaze disconcerting at first, but she talked about her experiences in a straightforward, nondefensive way. She told me she was a former heroin addict and had been on her own since she was fifteen. She dropped out of school in the ninth grade, after having been "kicked out" of her father's house. When she applied to the CETA program at the Southeast center, Jean had been "clean" for nearly a year and was receiving temporary income support from the Children's Services Division in Portland.

Peggy Bromfield was an eighteen-year-old welfare mother. She has thick, curly brown hair and is pretty, despite her jagged front teeth, about which she was noticeably self-conscious. There was still an adolescent air in the way that Peggy talked and moved, and it was difficult at first to believe that she was the mother of two toddlers. The oldest of five children herself, Peggy was raised in a two-parent, working-class family. She became pregnant for the first time at fifteen and dropped out of the ninth grade to marry her twenty-six-year-old boyfriend. She was pregnant with her second child when she and her husband split up the following year. Peggy said she had been enrolled in a CETA medical careers project for about two months.

Just three months short of his twentieth birthday, *Todd Clinton* was the oldest teen-ager I interviewed from Portland's Southeast center. Though he was still enrolled in cosmetology school as a CETA participant, Todd's cordial manner and new-wave haircut and clothes conveyed the image of a professional hair stylist. Todd told me that his first job had been in construction. He was only thirteen when he started working with his father, who owns a small fiberglass construction company in Portland. His father made it clear that he expected Todd to take over the business one day. But Todd never liked construction work and wanted to do something different with his life. The two had violent arguments. When Todd was seventeen, he dropped out of high school and left home to join the National Guard. When he got back to Portland, he could not find a job and went back to working with his father. Though their fighting resumed, they worked together for more than a year before Todd decided that he had to quit and train himself for a different line of work. Todd came to the CETA program when his father refused to lend him the money for cosmetology school. He told me:

> When I finally decided to go to cosmetology school, it was very rough. I quit my dad when he said he needed me most. He wouldn't lend me the money for school. Hell, when he found out I was in *cosmetology* school, he didn't even want me to come in his house! I guess the macho son image was just *blown* when I picked hair design.

We're All Looking for Something

> We're all here for *somethin'*—findin' out what we can do as far as
> workin' goes—lookin' for a way to get started. In some ways, I'm no
> different from anyone else in this program—in the world, really. But
> what I think and how it's been for me is probably real different
> from some of the other people you might talk to. There's all dif-
> ferent kinds of people in here, you know? And no two people you
> could talk to would probably be quite the same. We're all lookin'
> for somethin'—but it might be different things. Everybody's got
> their own story. Everybody's got their own ideas.   *Sandy Bonds*

Sandy was right: No two young people whom I interviewed were
quite alike. I quickly discovered that I was dealing with people rather than
stereotypes. There were similar patterns in the circumstances of the young
people, the problems they faced, and their reasons for enrolling in CETA
programs. Each of the teen-agers in our group wanted to work. All of them
needed income to support themselves, and all felt they needed help to get a
good start in the working world. The range in their ages was not wide: the
youngest, Luanne Clawson, turned seventeen before the interviews began;
the oldest, Todd Clinton, had not yet reached his twentieth birthday. But
similarities within the group were overshadowed by differences in the
backgrounds, personalities, and aspirations of the young people.

Differences in race, family background, and geographic setting were
most apparent. Of the seven young people from Boston, all but two were
black. Bobby, Adam, Harold, Genetta and Luanne had spent all or part of
their lives in public-housing projects, where nearly all of their neighbors
were black; and each of them came from households that depended on
welfare payments as the primary source of income. Felisa Santana came
from a large, welfare-dependent Puerto Rican family that lived in a mixed
neighborhood. Sven Latoka came from a white, working-class family in
Jamaica Plain.

Two of the young people from Kalamazoo, Carrie and Jack, were
white. Carrie came from a working-class family. Jack's family had depended
on welfare on an intermittent basis. Carmeletta DeVries, also from Kalamazoo, was black. Her mother had been on welfare throughout most of
Carmeletta's adolescence.

Of the six young people from Portland, only two, Jean and Sandy
(both white), had spent part of their childhood in welfare-dependent households. Peggy Bromfield, the other young white woman from Portland,
grew up in a large, low-income family. Todd Clinton, who was white, and
Douglas Giscard, whose family origins were French Canadian and Native

American, both came from middle-income homes. Tien Van Chin came from an Indo-Chinese family that had been relatively well-off until the fall of Saigon.

Stable, two-parent family backgrounds were rare among the young people in our group. Only six of these teen-agers had parents who were married and still living together. Some of the young people had been on their own from the time they were fourteen or fifteen, and the majority were living on their own during the period in which the interviews were held. Only three, Adam, Felisa, and Luanne, had lived continuously at home. Three of the young women, Genetta, Carmeletta, and Peggy, were single parents heading their own households.

All of the young people left the public school system before high school graduation. The years of education attained before they dropped out ranged from nine to nearly twelve, but the variation in their academic ability was great. Bobby Jones bordered on functional illiteracy. Sandy Bonds was a voracious reader but had almost no mathematical competency. Tien Van Chin had received the equivalent of a good secondary education but had limited reading and writing skills in English. Some of the young people, such as Sven, Luanne, and Carrie, said they had been slow learners in school. Others, such as Harold, Douglas, and Jean, had demonstrated good academic abilities during their early years in school. But none of the young people in our group had been able to function well in a high school classroom setting.

Their work experience was also varied. Some of the young people —Sven, Jack, Carrie, and Tien—had a number of different jobs before enrolling in CETA programs. Others—Bobby, Luanne, Sandy, and Carmeletta—had little or no work experience. Most had either been out of the labor force altogether or had been looking for work for at least six months before getting CETA-subsidized work, but several left jobs in the private sector to participate in youth programs.

Despite these disparities, none of the young people in our group were satisfied with the kind of work they could get on their own. None of them were able to break out of the part-time, unskilled job market into the world of full-time, adult employment. Although a few, such as Sven and Todd, had already made tentative career choices before coming into CETA programs, most did not know what they wanted to do or even what possibilities there were for them in the world of work.

The young people in our group were facing entry into the full-time work force, but they were hardly at the beginning. The development of a working life or career is a continual and individual process. A single or simple formula for success does not exist. Young people seeking to establish productive lives start off from different places, with diverse needs and expectations, which they attempt to meet in different ways. Though the first full-time job is a benchmark—whether it comes at age sixteen, nineteen, or twenty-five—it can hardly be viewed as a beginning, or as an end. The development of a career begins with the early experience and learning that take place in the home, neighborhood, school, and community; and it continues with the vocational and personal experiences, achievements, or setbacks that transpire throughout adult life.

Before we follow the young people through their CETA program experiences and consider their future employment prospects, let us hear what they have to say about their family lives and the roles they played in their communities and schools.

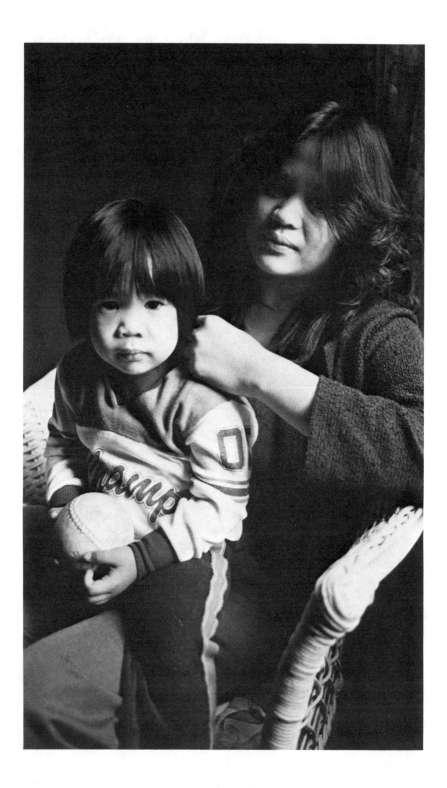

2. Family Life

The Ideal Family

> I'll tell you what I always wanted most. God, it sounds really dumb,
> but I always just wanted a normal family—a mother and father who
> always cared about you, you know?—a normal family that grows up
> together—like you see on TV—all those families that *talk* to each
> other—brothers and sisters that really talk and were always
> concerned about one another—you know what I mean? I always
> thought that would be the ideal way to live; you know, the baby
> grew up and had no problems!   *Jean Ansel*

Jean laughed after she said, "The baby grew up and had no problems."
At seventeen, she no longer really believes in ideal families or "happy-ever-
after." She knows that people from even the happiest and most secure
families have problems. But she does not laugh when she talks about
growing up in her own family. The problems that she faced as a child still
seem very real:

> Our family life was pretty terrible. I knew it was bad—even when I
> was little—but I didn't know why it had to be like that. See, my
> mother always had a drinking problem. My parents fought all the
> time real bad, and they finally split up when I was in the sixth grade.
> After that I kept living back and forth between my mother and my
> father. Neither one of them really wanted me in their homes
> because I was too much of a problem, they thought. So it was like
> they were pushing me back and forth all the time. I first got
> involved with drugs when I was twelve. I think I started taking pills
> just to get their attention, you know? But it didn't work, 'cause then
> they just got disgusted and turned against me even more.

Jean isn't sure who or what to blame for the way things turned out
in her family, but she believes that she has had to pay for it. Her self-image,
health, education, and aspirations have all suffered because of her family
life. For Jean, and for many of the other young people I interviewed, the
contrast between the image of an ideal family and the reality of her own
family experiences is sharp and painful.

Most of the young people in our group seemed to grow up with vivid fantasies of the ideal family, based on traditional middle-class values and assumptions and fleshed out by television. Though some of them can laugh now about their romantic notions, they are often able to describe the ideal family in great detail and are still inclined to measure their own family experiences against this mythical norm.

According to these young people, a "normal" family includes at least two children with two parents who love each other and stay married. The father works in an "office" and earns enough money so that the family can have the things they need, as well as the extras that make life enjoyable. The mother generally stays home to attend to the household and raise the children. These normal families do things together. The parents may have to scold and even enforce occasional punishment for misbehavior, but they enjoy spending time with their children and are always there to help and encourage them to do their best. The brothers and sisters may sometimes argue and tease, but they like each other and are willing to join forces to help each other out. When problems crop up, these ideal families *talk* about them; and they are always able, somehow, to work things out together.

While financial security figured largely in the ideal-family images of the teen-agers who came from low-income homes, it is the concept of family solidarity, mutual support, and togetherness that this group of young people seemed most attracted to and missed most in their own experiences. Stable, two-parent families are becoming less common in American society. An estimated four out of ten children born in the 1970s are spending at least part of their childhoods in a single-parent household. The majority of the young people in our group came from families split by divorce, death, or desertion. By their accounts, the parent or adult left with responsibility for the children was often too beset by personal and financial pressures to provide the kind of care they needed and craved. Young people such as Jean, Sandy, Jack, and Carrie felt more neglected than abused. They talked about the lack of communication, caring, and together-ness in their family lives. They felt cut off from their parents, but were not really able to blame them for their lack of attention and support. Early in life, they seemed to realize that their parents faced problems of their own, which left them without the energy, perspective, or ability to play a con-sistent, guiding role in their children's lives.

Jack Thrush, the Kalamazoo participant who seemed so wary and elusive, told me that his family lived precariously for a number of years after his father died. His mother was a waitress when she could find work; in between jobs, the family depended on welfare. Jack's older brother,

Dan, took care of him most of the time. The two brothers were close until Dan enlisted in the army and left home when Jack was fifteen. Jack believes that life was especially hard for his mother after his father's death. She had several unhappy relationships with other men and finally remarried the year that Dan left home. Jack felt like a burden in the new family created by his mother and stepfather. He left home the next year at sixteen when he got his first job.

Less than a year later, unemployed and without funds, Jack moved back into the house. But things were not much better and he did not plan to stay long:

> I prefer not to live at home, but I guess it's the best I can do for now. It's clean and there's usually enough food and everything, but my mother—uh, I don't know. They don't really *need* me there or anything. She and my stepdad are real busy and usually hassled, so they don't have time to talk much or get very involved. Ever since my dad died, my mother and me don't communicate much. We didn't fight or anything; but we never did stuff together, and she hardly got involved in my life at all. Sometimes I wish we could be more of—like a *unit* or something. But my mom's been through a lot—that's more or less what it is—and it's like she just can't afford to get involved or something. Sometimes my stepdad will try to talk to me, but you know he never really gives me advice or tells me what's really going on with him. Maybe he just doesn't want to get me involved in his problems.

Sandy Bonds is another of the young people who felt her mother was too absorbed by problems in her own life to respond adequately to her children's needs. Sandy's parents divorced when she was in the third grade. She spent some time in a foster home, but she was living with her mother in Maryland when she first started getting into serious trouble at school. Her mother decided she was not able to handle her, and Sandy took off for Arizona to live with her father. Sandy has tried to look at the situation from her mother's perspective:

> I know I wanted more attention, but I don't think it was really my mother's fault. She had a lot of problems of her own, you know. I don't know all that much about her background, but she was a foster kid herself. I think she dropped out of school in the eighth grade. She always had financial problems. See, at first my family had a lot of money. They were middle, or upper-middle class, I guess you might say. Then when my father left, we dropped down to lower class—like that! Later, my stepfather.was a truck driver, and that business was kinda slow.

There's lots of things my mother didn't teach us—stuff we should've learned about getting along in the world and how to handle ourselves. It was like she wasn't there half the time or something. But I don't think it was her fault. In her own strange way, I think she cared about us kids. She wouldn't ever tell us what we should do, but she'd always say, you know, "Look at *me*—you can do better for yourselves." She wasn't much on understanding what was going on with me or the rest of the family—neither of my parents were. When a problem arose, my parents would just—sort of—well, they just didn't understand the problems. And they didn't know how to solve them anyway. And neither did I.

Several of the young people had been living for a number of years in households where neither parent was present. When Harold Thomas's stable family life in Virginia was destroyed by the death of his parents, he and his younger brother and sisters were taken in by an older sister in Boston. Harold says she had her hands full just working and keeping food on the table, so he tried to help out with the younger ones as much as he could.

Bobby Jones also lives in a public-housing project in Boston with his older sister and younger siblings. He spent his early years in a single-parent household and says he cannot remember ever seeing his father. Bobby was fourteen years old when his mother died. Janice, Bobby's older sister, was only nineteen, but she assumed responsibility for the three other Jones children. Bobby says that he appreciates what his sister has done, but that she was not really able to take the place of a parent:

Janice's done the best she could for us; I know that. But it was never like—well, things were better when my mother was livin'. I went to school then, played around outside after school, came inside at a certain time, done my homework—you know, that was it! I never was really like hangin' in the streets back then. Well, maybe in the summer I was sometimes in the streets, you know. But I never really got bad then. I could control myself, keep myself out of trouble.

When my mother died, I never really felt—uh—It really hurt me when she passed away. But, you know, it seemed to everyone like I was the kind of person, I could get over it real quick. And after awhile, I just didn't think about it. I depended on *myself*—you know, I never really fell back on nobody.

Janice, you know, it just seemed like she couldn't really tell me what to do. I mean, she always just *tried* to tell me, you know, stuff like "Go to school," "Get *in* something." But it just washed over me. If I wanted to do somethin', I wouldn't *ask* her about it; I would *tell* her what it was or just go ahead and *do* it.

Even among the smaller group of young people from two-parent families, the emotional quality of family life rarely matched the cheerful, cooperative climate that they imagined to prevail in "normal" families. While some of the youngsters suffered from a lack of parental support and guidance, others had parents who had been repressively strict and critical, or even abusive, toward them. In several cases, parents had exercised such restrictive controls that their children were cut off from experiences and relationships outside the family.

Peggy Bromfield's parents married young. Her father was a construction worker whose employment fluctuated with the ups and downs of Portland's housing industry. A new baby coming almost every year put strains on the Bromfields' marriage. Peggy's mother had trouble controlling her temper. As the oldest child, with a strong temper of her own, Peggy was often the target for her mother's anger:

> It would happen sometimes with all the kids, but she used to beat me most. My mom always told everyone that she doesn't really like kids at all. So I've always wondered, you know, why did she have five of them?
>
> My mom and dad were always really tight on us. They didn't like us to go to friends' houses like kids do. I wasn't allowed to spend the night at a girlfriend's or anything like that. And they didn't like to have people in the house, so I was hardly ever allowed to have friends over. I hardly had friends anyway. I always felt like there was somethin' wrong with me. They were always criticizing me. It was like they were waitin' for me to make a mistake.
>
> I didn't understand then why they were like that. But lookin' back, I think they were probably just scared that somethin' bad would happen or that they would do somethin' wrong. My mom got married when she was fifteen. By the time she was twenty-two, she had five kids to take care of. She told me she didn't want us to ruin our lives like she did hers. But they were so strict with me that I ended up doing everything behind their back. Them being so over-protective didn't prepare me for life at all. I was the first one to leave. I got married at fifteen, and after that they eased up a little with the rest of the kids.

Todd Clinton also grew up in a two-parent family in Portland. Todd's father earned a good living, and the family never suffered from material deprivation. Todd thinks his father cared about the family, and he did teach Todd how to work. But Mr. Clinton's bouts of drinking and sporadic violence and his constant verbal abuse made family life miserable for Todd:

My dad tried to run my life—just like his own. He's a hard worker, but he's obsessed by money and he drinks too much. When I was around, his whole life was just surrounded on, more or less, giving me a hard time. It was like kidding to him, but it didn't seem like kidding. He expected so much out of me when I worked with him. He rode me all the time. I just couldn't take all the riding. He was always getting mad—beating me down. I was sinking. Finally I felt it was either him or—I mean, I *knew* I had to get out of there.

While the majority of these young people sought an early escape from family lives they viewed as oppressive, chaotic, or empty, there were several among the sixteen who were still living at home and who felt generally satisfied with the quality of their family lives. Felisa Santana, Sven Latoka, and Luanne Clawson all came from families that had been through hard times. None of their families fit the ideal image. Moving between Puerto Rico and Boston, from periods of low-paying work to times of unemployment and welfare recipiency, the Santanas struggle to support a family of eight. After years of self-employment as a carpenter, Sven Latoka's father faced a period when there was no demand for his work, and he had to leave home and hire out on a fishing-boat crew to keep the family going. The Clawsons lived in a public-housing project in Boston. Luanne's parents were separated and the family depended on welfare for support. But despite the misfortunes and material limitations of their lives, the young people from these three families admired their parents and felt they had done a good job raising them. All three had reached the age when they felt responsible for themselves and wanted to help their parents. Though they looked forward to a more independent life outside the family, they were relatively happy at home and planned to stay there until they had the job security and financial resources to strike out on their own.

What do these young people say about their family lives? How do their experiences differ from those of the teenagers who left home? During our second interview, Sven talked about his life at home:

SL I've liked living at home. My parents are fine—no arguments with them, you know. Soon, I expect, I'll be moving out on my own—not until I've got a better job, though.

BS Do you make a financial contribution to the house?

SL Yeah, yeah. I have to pay room and board—thirty dollars a week.

BS Does that seem reasonable to you?

SL Yeah. Yeah, it does. That's one reason I haven't moved out yet—on my own I'd have to pay more. It would cost quite a bit more for me to live away from home.

BS If you're making a decision about a job or something else that's important to you, would your parents get involved?

SL Yeah, they help me a lot. Now I'm of age, you know, I'm a man; and I basically take care of my own. But I'd let 'em know for sure, like, yeah, like if I was up for a job. They have anything to say to me, they probably would speak right up. They don't stop me from doin' what I want; they wouldn't do *that*. They think I'm doin' something wrong, though, they'd tell me about it.

BS If you have children, do you think you'll raise them very much as you've been raised?

SL Yeah. I'll be strict—firm—'cause I think they'll be better off for it in the long run.

BS You think your parents were strict?

SL Yeah. I know they were. I always knew from them what you *should* do and what you *shouldn't* do. But they didn't use force. My father's hit me a couple times in my life. I was never beat. But when I did something wrong, I knew it. And I had ground rules—come in at a certain time and stuff like that. If I didn't come in, I couldn't go out the next time—smarten up to it, you know? When I was younger, I had an allowance. I had to earn that too. Taking out the rubbish when it had to be, uh, fixing things, working around the house.

BS Why do you think that kind of upbringing is good?

SL For one thing, I learned to work. How to do a job. And, well, when I see all the kids who were out all night when they were young, and I take a look at 'em now, they don't seem to be doin' very well. I'm not doin' great; I've had my troubles finding jobs. But I figure I'm just about one step ahead of anybody that's had no—I guess you'd say, no *discipline*. I had a curfew until I was eighteen. Since I was old enough, I had some kind of job—at least part-time. And I been pretty independent. My parents let me make a lot of my own decisions, but they taught me that you have to do *certain* things. You have to keep a good attitude about yourself in order to have a decent attitude towards other people.

Parental support, discipline, and responsibility were key elements in what Sven viewed, with justification, as a successful family life. His parents were not only able to set and enforce reasonable standards of behavior, they were willing to give Sven the freedom to make choices and accept responsibility for his own actions. Very few of the other young people's parents seemed to have been able to do this effectively, though Luanne Clawson's experience indicates that it can be done under even more adverse circumstances. Luanne's mother was raising three children alone on welfare, but she managed to transmit to her daughter both a workable set of values and a sense of responsibility and self-worth. Luanne says:

> I'd try to do just like my mother—if I had kids. 'Cause my mother's doing hard things, you know. Trying to make it, tries to give us money for the things we need, makes us good clothes to wear—just everything. I know my mother is really concerned about me. She's taught me a lot. You know, she tells me things I need to know about when I get out on my own. You have to get out there and work, pay your bills on time, and stuff like that. She wants me to really make something out of my life, you know? So I feel like I won't really have no problems doin' what I want—long as I come to her first and let her know what I'm gonna do. I decide, but I still like to know what she thinks.
>
> If I had kids of my own, I'd raise 'em just like I was. Yes, I would, really. I'd teach 'em right from wrong. I'd tell 'em, you know, "Don't do such and such a thing." But I wouldn't keep naggin' them about it. After I told them, you know, if they feel that they can make up their own minds on it, I'd let 'em go. But there's *certain* things —*some* things, I'd make 'em go by my rules—what I say—at least while they're livin' with me.

Out on Our Own

The vast majority—more than 90 percent—of Americans under eighteen years old live at home with at least one parent. But among our sixteen young people, there were only two who had not tried life on their own before their eighteenth birthdays. Some chose to leave their families; others felt they were pushed out. A few were seeking an adventure or temporary respite from problems at school or at home. But most felt their family circumstances were untenable, and they were looking for a better life. How does a fourteen-, fifteen-, or sixteen-year-old go about leaving home? Where do they go? And what happens to them once they are out on their own?

Douglas Giscard left home near the end of his fifteenth year because of family conflicts. When I met him, he had been on his own for nearly three years. He was a serious and articulate young man with long black hair tied back neatly in a ponytail. "You might not believe this," Douglas told me, with a laugh, "but my long hair had a lot to do with my leaving home." He described his family as "pretty well-off, conservative middle-class people." His father, a French Canadian immigrant, was the manager of a drugstore in Portland. His mother, who grew up on a Suquamish Indian reservation, was a full-time homemaker. Douglas has two younger brothers, who were still living at home. His parents are devout Catholics, but Douglas said he had been an agnostic since he was twelve.

When he was living at home, Douglas was required to go to church every Sunday, attend a strict Catholic school, be in the house by nine o'clock each night, and keep his hair trimmed above the earlobes. His objections to these rules led to a series of drawn-out struggles with his father. Douglas told me how their conflict was resolved:

> We were fightin' all the time, and it was hard on everyone. I could
> see that, but I couldn't give up my values. And finally I decided that
> I had to go. My dad and I agreed that it was fine with both of us
> that I was leaving. In fact, for me to move out was the only thing we
> could think of to do. I moved in with a roommate—a guy I knew
> who was eighteen and had an apartment. And my dad agreed to
> give me $100 a month, so I'd go my way and live my own life. He
> may have expected to see me change my mind and come back, but
> I knew I was out for good.

In some ways, Douglas was prepared to be on his own. He was used to doing chores around the house; and when he moved in with his older friend, Gil, he didn't find it hard to cook, clean up, and take care of himself. He saw his parents occasionally and felt his relationship with his father had improved some after he left home. Douglas said he enjoyed the privacy and feeling of independence, but he soon found that the $100 a month his parents were willing to give him wouldn't stretch far enough to cover his expenses.

He spent some time looking for a part-time job but couldn't find anything that would fit in with his school schedule. His roommate, Gil, was going to community college and dealing drugs to support himself. Douglas got involved in dealing—mostly marijuana. After several months, he quit school and they expanded the business. Douglas and Gil started branching out; together they planned and executed a number of successful burglaries. For nearly two years, they lived well off the proceeds of their illegal activities. Douglas said that it started as "kind of a joke." He never really saw himself as a criminal, but it was an easy way to make money—until he got caught. In 1978 Douglas was arrested while leaving the scene of a burglary with $2,000 worth of antique watches and jewelry in his pockets. The juvenile court allowed Douglas to remain on his own, but he was placed on probation and ordered to find employment so that he could pay the court fees.

Jean Ansel, the young woman who said she always wanted a "normal family," was not yet fifteen when she left home. Jean had started taking barbiturates when she was only twelve. She got drugs from older "friends" she met hanging around the park near her mother's home. Her mother decided she could not handle her, and Jean was living with her father and his girlfriend when she started using heroin at age fourteen. Neither of her parents was prepared to help Jean with her drug problems:

> When I was hooked on downers, the only reactions I ever got from my father were just—well, *nothing,* really. There was no communication going on at all. Sometimes they would tell me how stupid I was and stuff like that. But there was no real caring. They never made no effort to say anything, like: "Why don't you stop?," "You need help," "Can I help you?," or anything like that. And that's what I wanted to hear before I could tell myself to stop. When I got into heroin, my father had to know it—like he'd be findin' needles and stuff. He always went into my bedroom and he would find the needles. I would say I wasn't usin' it, and he'd yell at me but he wouldn't do anything. Then, the last night that I lived there, he made me show my arms. That proved it right there, and that's when he kicked me out.

When Jean left her father's house with needle marks on both arms, she was in for several really rough years. But at first things looked as if they might work out reasonably well. Jean had a "straight" friend from school who knew of her addiction. This girl's parents sometimes took in foster children. Jean knew the family, and they had some understanding of her situation. They were able to make the necessary arrangements to have Jean placed in their home as a foster child. The foster family was stable and supportive. They saw Jean through her withdrawal from heroin. But, ironically, Jean found she was unable to sustain herself in the "normal" family situation she had always craved:

> They were really wonderful people—all of them. And they really stuck by me and helped me out a lot. But, like, that was in February, and come June, I just couldn't handle living there. They were the nicest people I had ever known. And I know it was my fault, but it was just *too* much of a family situation. Um, you know, like they had the mother, the father, the kids—a complete family. And I hadn't been used to that. Even when my family was together, we weren't like that. They were all so much *nicer* than me. It made me feel worse somehow. I didn't know how to act. I didn't belong. It was just like—it was just *too straight.*

It was really hard to leave, but I knew I had to get up and go. I told them I was going to try it again at my father's house. And I went back there for like two weeks. I tried to do it at my father's, but it didn't work at all. It was weird; I really couldn't make it there, but it seemed like that was where I belonged.

Then I was staying at a friend's house. And I started seein' a drug counselor at this rehabilitation place. I was mostly drinkin' then instead of doing drugs. And she—my drug counselor—put me in this shelter home. I stayed there for awhile. And from there, I hit the streets.

Um, out on the streets—I wasn't workin'. It's kind of a blank time for me. How was I gettin' money? Well, I knew people—I think—I was sorta doing odd jobs, I guess. [pause] I hate to admit it, but I was also hustling—doing tricks—and I was shootin' up again, but not as much as before, and drinkin'. That whole time I can't remember too well, and I don't like to remember it either. It went on, on and off, for over a year.

Finally, Jean took steps to get herself off the streets. She contacted the Children's Services Division in Portland. They were able to put her on their independent-living program, which provides temporary support payments to minors, living away from home, who are willing to go to school and look for work.

When Tien Van Chin left his home in Saigon in 1975 he was only fourteen years old. The South Vietnamese government had been disbanded, the North Vietnamese were taking over, and the city was in chaos. Tien's school was shut down. Food was scarce, he said. Crowds of people were living in the streets and lining up at warehouses for rice. People like Tien's parents—who owned a plastics manufacturing plant that had supplied the South Vietnamese army—were making arrangements to flee the country. The Van Chins paid about $400 in gold to the owners of a small fishing-boat to ensure that Tien, their oldest surviving son, would get out of the country. Although their own prospects were poor under the new regime, the older Chins decided to remain in Saigon. Tien said:

> My parents stayed. When you live somewhere too many years, you don't want to just left there. You can't go and just leave your assets. My parents let me go. They understand I make a chance by myself. When they turn the country over to Viet Cong, I know I will not be able to learn a good occupation. That's why I go. I took a choice to come here. Growing up, I have hear a lot of the United States. I believe it is best place for young people—to come here, learn to get ahead for themselves.

Tien celebrated his fifteenth and sixteenth birthdays in a refugee camp. After two years at the camp in Thailand, he finally made it to the United States. Tien was relocated in Portland under the sponsorship of a church agency. He was seventeen years old and wanted to go to the university. But he had no money and his English was poor, so he began a series of factory and restaurant jobs while he studied English at night. He lived in a cooperative household with five other young Indo-Chinese men. Three of the younger boys were going to high school and working part-time. The two older ones were working full-time. None was making over minimum wage, but they pooled their earnings and shared housekeeping duties. Among the group of young refugees, Tien's English was the best, so he handled most of the household business.

Most of the young people who struck out on their own at age sixteen or younger thought they were leaving home for good. For some of them, such as Tien, going back would have been impossible. Some were able to support themselves by legitimate means. Some, such as Sandy Bonds and Jean Ansel, chose the risks of street life over the more familiar pressures of their family lives. But others, within our group of young people, returned to their parents' houses when they found they could not make it on their own.

Two of the young people from Kalamazoo—Carrie Green and Jack Thrush—used the income from their first jobs to escape from unhappy lives at home and at school. Both were sixteen at the time—though Carrie lied about her age to get her job. Both moved out of their parents' homes and into apartments with friends. But neither was able to sustain an independent life for long. Carrie lost her factory job when her boss discovered her true age. Her friends helped her out for a while; but after two months without work, she had to move back to her father's house. This pattern was repeated several times over the next twenty months as Carrie found and lost job after job. Though Jack's first job lasted only a few months, he found other work and was able to stay out on his own for nearly a year. Both Carrie and Jack were unemployed and living at home when they signed up for CETA work at the youth program agency in Kalamazoo.

Three of the young men, Harold Thomas, Sven Latoka, and Todd Clinton, enlisted in the military at age seventeen. Ineligible, or unwilling to commit themselves to a full two-year term, none of them had signed up for regular duty. All three had dropped out of high school, were having trouble finding good jobs, and were eager to get away from home and see the world. Sven, whose older brother was a marine on active duty, joined the marine reserves and spent several months at a training camp in Virginia. He began studying for his GED examination at the camp, but he learned no skills that would directly improve his employment status when he returned to Boston. Harold Thomas, eager to escape the economic and racial pressures of Boston, enlisted in the army reserves. He was sent to boot camp in Georgia. Harold liked army life and considered signing on for regular duty, but he felt obligated to return to Boston to help his sisters and brother.

Todd Clinton saw the National Guard as a way to break out of the cycle of conflicts with his father and to escape a possible lifetime of involvement in the family's fiberglass construction business. Todd was stationed in Georgia for his seven months' active duty with the Guard, and he viewed this as an important and productive period in his life. In addition to combat training, Todd received academic instruction and was able to pass his GED examinations. Being away from home was good for Todd. He said: "It made me grow up. It made me realize a lot of things, and I was able to accept myself more." Todd was the only one of the three young men who enlisted who received occupational training while in the military:

> See, when I went in the Guard I had the idea that I wanted to be a disc jockey—'cause I talked a lot. So they sent me to this school for training disc jockeys, and I did okay. I got my third-class license. I was thinkin' at first that this could be a job for me when I got out. But I found out there that there's more disc jockeys than there is jobs. And I realized that I didn't have any special thing for it that a lot of others don't have. It wasn't really my talent, so I decided not to do it. See, I'm the kind of person, I don't necessarily have to be the best, but I don't want to be real lousy—or even mediocre either.

Todd's experience in the National Guard was positive. He got a chance to study and to learn more about himself and the world of work. He grew, but, like Harold and Sven, he returned home to find that little had changed.

Adolescent Parents

Three of the young women who left home at an early age were mothers raising children on their own. Despite the increased availability of birth control information and devices, the incidence of pregnancy among young unmarried women has increased dramatically in the past fifteen years. An estimated one out of ten teen-aged girls in the United States becomes pregnant each year. The number of pregnant teen-agers who choose to bear and raise their children is also rising. Adolescent, single parenthood is being chosen by a growing number of young women. Who are these young women embarking upon motherhood in their teens? How do they view their lives as single parents?

Genetta Burke is nineteen years old and lives in Dorchester with her four-and-a-half year-old son, three-year-old daughter, and grandmother. She grew up in the Victoria Point housing project, where her mother still lives and where Genetta now reports for work on the weatherization project. Genetta was the oldest of seven children. Her mother supported the family through a combination of work and welfare—a pattern that Genetta herself has followed. Genetta's parents are married, but her father has spent most of his life in North Carolina.

The boy who was to become the father of Genetta's children also grew up in Victoria Point. The two started dating when Genetta was thirteen. Genetta was not yet fifteen when she became pregnant for the first time, and she had been sexually active for less than a year. She was still in high school and had not planned to get pregnant, but Genetta says she did not have to think long about her decision to keep the baby: "When it happens, it happens. I always wanted kids *someday,* so I figgered I might as well start now."

But Genetta and her nineteen-year-old boyfriend, Virgil, were not ready to get married. While Genetta was still in the hospital after giving birth to a son, her mother made arrangements for her to receive an Aid to Families with Dependent Children (AFDC) grant, and Genetta and her baby lived with her mother for nearly a year. Then Genetta left home to live with Virgil—first at his mother's house and later, when they could afford to buy furniture, in an apartment of their own. Shortly after their daughter was born, Genetta asked Virgil to move out of the apartment to make room for her elderly grandmother. Since then, Genetta has been the head of her own household. She receives welfare checks and Virgil generally gives her $25 to $30 a week extra to cover expenses. Though she still sees Virgil regularly and considers him her boyfriend, Genetta has no immediate plans for marriage:

> I'm chicken. I don't wanna get married yet, 'cause I don't think
> marriage is for everybody. You know, when you're young and you
> get married, you usually break up. My kids' father, he wants to
> marry me. But I think that he just wants to marry me so he can
> keep me stayin' in the house. [laughter] He can't tell me what to
> do now, 'cause we don't stay together. But if we was to get married,
> you know, he would wanna live together; and I'm too independent
> for that. I think I'm better off on my own for now. I'll get married
> someday, when the right man comes along.

Carmeletta DeVries got pregnant several months before her sixteenth birthday. She was in the tenth grade and lived with her mother in Kalamazoo. Carmeletta did not have a positive view of the life of a single parent. Her parents had separated when Carmeletta was in grade school.

Though her father still lived in Kalamazoo and she saw him fairly often, Carmeletta said he did not help the family out much financially. Her mother had moved on and off the welfare rolls as she struggled to raise her children by herself. Carmeletta's older sister had become a welfare mother while she was still in her teens, and her life alone with two toddlers did not look easy or attractive to Carmeletta. But she decided to go ahead with the pregnancy, although, unlike many of the other young women I interviewed, she was not looking forward to being a mother.

Though, as a rule, their pregnancies were unplanned, and they realized that their youth, relative inexperience, and lack of a husband raised problems that might be difficult to solve, many of the teen-aged mothers I interviewed seemed to have viewed impending parenthood with surprisingly positive expectations. From the time they were first pregnant, most of these young women had equated abortion with "killing your baby," and had not considered it a viable alternative. But Carmeletta had chosen abortion before, when she was fourteen and pregnant for the first time. And she considered abortion as a possible solution during her second unplanned pregnancy:

> My parents told me I could have an abortion if I wanted, you know? 'Cause being pregnant was messing up my life. I mean, I didn't *need* any baby. But I had got pregnant once before and I had an abortion then. And I felt like I couldn't—You can't just keep on having abortions, you know? Sometimes I felt sorry about the first one. It was sad, you know? I was fourteen or something like that and I just couldn't deal with it. My boyfriend was mad at me for getting rid of it, but there was no way I could handle a baby then.
>
> This time my father sit down and explain it to me—all the facts or whatever about getting an abortion—just what the choices were. And I understood 'em, you know. And I decided to go ahead and have the baby. But it wasn't that I felt it was the *right* choice or anything like that; I just had to have it. You can't just keep goin' on with abortions—it wouldn't be right.

Carmeletta did not think much about marriage. Her boyfriend, Eddie, did not have a steady job and was not interested in being tied down. Like Genetta, Carmeletta lived with her mother until after her son was born. The two argued over whether Eddie should be allowed to stay overnight in the house when he visited Carmeletta and the baby. Hoping to move out and find a place of her own, Carmeletta applied for AFDC. She was given only a partial allotment as she was considered to still be her mother's dependent. Her older sister, eager for company and for someone to help out around the house, asked Carmeletta to move in with her. Carmeletta preferred living at her sister's house to staying with her mother, but she was not really satisfied with the arrangement:

> Stayin' at my sister's really isn't that good for me. It's not like we fight or anything, but it's *her* place and she has the say. I don't like the way she keeps her house or does with her kids, but I can't really say much about it, you know? If Eddie come over, it's okay with her. But it's crowded—there's hardly room there for all *her* stuff. And the kids are always cryin' and everything.

Peggy Bromfield was living in Portland with her parents and four brothers and sisters when she became pregnant. It was the summer after the ninth grade, and Peggy was almost fifteen years old. Peggy says that she was not unhappy when she realized she was pregnant. Unlike Carmeletta, Peggy wanted very much to have a baby and was convinced that she could handle it. She had technicolor fantasies of herself as a mother:

> I always wanted to have my kids while I was young. I never thought about marriage all that much, but I thought a lot about having a baby. I could just see myself . . . walking down the beach—looking real good—got my little girl on my hand, you know? She'd be about three years old—with curly, curly hair—We'd be smiling and talking. . . .

Though Peggy's fantasies did not necessarily include a husband, she was the only one of the three who married during her pregnancy. Genetta and Carmeletta, who did not seriously consider marriage during their pregnancies or immediately after their children were born, have both been keeping steady company with the young men who fathered their children since they first entered their teens. Peggy knew the man who was to become her husband for only a few months before she became pregnant. She had not been allowed to date much, and he was her first real boyfriend.

Before their pregnancies, none of the young women had any sexual experience outside of their relationships with these young men. They had only a vague understanding of birth control techniques and were willing to leave any responsibility in this area to their boyfriends. The three boyfriends, who were four to eleven years older than the young women, all seemed to have been rather pleased at the prospect of fatherhood—though their notions of what the role entailed were limited. In pursuing their relationships with these young men, each of the young women knew that pregnancy was a risk.

While both Genetta and Carmeletta were experiencing problems at school and were eager to establish more adult lives, only Peggy was really desperate to get away from home. She saw marriage as the best way to

escape an unhappy family life and admits that she deliberately used pregnancy as a means to gain her parents' approval for her marriage plans:

> At first I didn't think much of Larry; he was so much older, I
> couldn't see why he wanted to go out with me. But then he was so
> nice to me that I was really caring for him a lot. I felt if you really
> love each other enough, you want to make a baby together. And we
> figured we should show our love and how much we really wanted to
> be together. Startin' a kid is more of a bond, [though] my parents
> didn't like the idea of Larry bein' almost eleven years older than me.
> "Are you sure you know what you're doing?"—you know? But my
> mother had got married when she was fifteen, so she couldn't really
> say no because she did the same thing. My dad felt the same way
> too. And since they saw I was serious, they let me get married.

Soon after the wedding, Peggy's husband lost his job. "He claimed
that he couldn't find work," Peggy said. "But mostly he just sat home,
drinking; and he never wanted to let me go out of the house alone—even
to see my mother." When his unemployment checks ran out, Larry and
Peggy went on welfare. They conceived another child five months after
their first was born. The marriage lasted just over a year. When they
separated, Peggy was sixteen years old and five months pregnant.

Each of the three young women applied for AFDC after the birth of
her first baby, and all three were still receiving welfare support when they
enrolled in youth employment programs. This is a pattern I was to encounter many times. Nearly all of the several dozen teen-aged mothers I
interviewed had lived at home until their babies were born; few remained
with their parents for longer than a year after childbirth; and none managed
to get by on her own without AFDC support. AFDC grants allowed these
young mothers to move out of their parents' homes and into the adult
world—albeit on strained and restricted terms. The availability of AFDC
also seems to afford young women more sense of choice over the question
of marriage versus single parenthood.

While AFDC clearly helps to make single parenthood viable for adolescent women, I found no evidence that the availability of welfare payments acted as an *incentive* for early childbirth. Most of the teen-aged
mothers I talked to did not think very realistically about their financial
futures before or during their pregnancy. If anything, they tended to plan
naïvely that they would "go out and get a job somewhere" once the baby
was born. But few of them felt able to go to work and leave their infants
in the months immediately after childbirth. Those who did look for work
were usually discouraged when they found how few jobs they qualified for
and how little those jobs paid. AFDC was generally resorted to as the

easiest, most practical means of support when they decided that they needed to be away from their parents and on their own with their children.

How do these young women feel about their lives after their babies are born? Do they have any regrets? Most experienced difficulties—particularly during the first six months of motherhood. Meeting the needs and adjusting to the demands of an infant is a challenging experience for an adolescent girl. But there are moments of intense pride and exhilaration in mothering a "tiny baby who really needs you." Peggy, who started out with extremely positive expectations, said:

> My marriage was probably a mistake from the beginning. But I could never be sorry about havin' my kids. It's been real hard—doin' it mainly on my own—but I'm not sorry. It's one thing I've done that's *real*—nobody can take it away from me, you know? They're the most important thing in my life. I made some mistakes, but I think I done a pretty good job so far.

Carmeletta, whose view of prospective motherhood was far less positive, told me:

> It's a *whole* lot harder than I thought it would be. You get real tired—especially when he cries sometimes and you can't figure out what's wrong. I love him a lot—more than I thought I would, you know? But I ain't gonna have no more kids—that's for sure.

Genetta probably articulated best the mixed feelings of love, satisfaction, doubt, and regret experienced by a teen-aged mother:

> If I could do it over, I guess I wouldn't have any kids. Now that I, you know, *got* them, I love them—I wouldn't give them up for nobody. But if I could do it again—well, it would have been a lot easier without them. A lot of times, I've felt like I couldn't do stuff or enjoy myself because my kids were there. But then sometimes I think: Maybe there's really nothin' out there *to* do. You know, maybe I'm not really missing nothin'. 'Cause sometimes if you don't have nobody in your life, then it don't really mean nothin'. At least I always have my kids to cheer me up when I get depressed. I can talk with them, play with them. They can lift my spirits.
>
> If I could change things, I guess I wouldn't have sat home all the time I did—altogether, I sat home about three years—doin' nothin'. I wasted time. I didn't get no place. The only real part about it was my kids though. But I wish that, well, I should've finished high school—I mean when I was first there—but I don't know. You know, my mother said that I just don't have any sense. But you know, the thing was—I was just *young*. I was just tryin' to find out what life was about.

Role Models for Adult Life

Adult role models are important for a young person trying to put together an independent life. Observation, interaction, and identification with successful adults can help young people to develop self-confidence and to collect information and insights that can be put to use in making their own choices about life styles, values, and work. For most young people, parents serve as the primary role models. While few parents expect their children to follow exactly in their footsteps, and most parents play only an indirect role in vocational guidance and preparation, it is the intimate and sustained contact of family life that provides most youngsters with the knowledge, values, habits, and expectations that will guide their approach to work and personal life as adults.

Among our group of young people, family life was marked by instability and dissatisfying relations between parents and children. The employment experiences of their parents generally afforded little in the way of positive role models. Unsatisfying work, low pay, poor job security, unemployment, and welfare recipiency were common among the adults they knew. Only a minority of the young people had sustained contact with an adult who had managed to establish and maintain a productive work life.

Sven Latoka's experience in this area was far from typical for the group. Though his father had his share of employment difficulties, the Latoka family's relationships fit into a traditional pattern. Mr. Latoka was the breadwinner, while his wife stayed home to care for the children and manage the household. Sven's father, a second-generation Ukranian, was trained by his father to be a carpenter. For several decades he was steadily employed doing cabinetry and remodeling work in Jamaica Plain. Sven began going out on jobs and helping his father when he was only thirteen. After Sven dropped out of school the two worked together on a full-time basis, until work became scarce and Mr. Latoka worked temporarily as a fisherman. Sven admires his father and would like to follow in his footsteps:

> I *would* like to be like my father. I like his trade—he's a carpenter—and I like that. And, well, he's smart too. He knows what's right and what's wrong—you know, and you can't really get over on him. He's physically fit, and that I admire. Gives me sort of an example to get going myself. I think he's led a pretty good life—an interesting one. He's been in the army, he's traveled, and he's done good by his family—besides, he's my father!

Todd Clinton also began working with his father on construction jobs during his early teens. Mr. Clinton's fiberglass construction firm prospered, but the Clinton's family life was not as stable or happy as the Latoka's. Todd was eager to disassociate himself from his father and establish his own career in another field. Though he admires his father's financial success, Todd does not want to emulate him in other ways:

> I would like to have the money that my dad makes. I gotta hand it to him—he's made a lotta money. But he more or less keeps it all to himself. He's not happy, and he worries all the time. He doesn't broaden himself. He doesn't want his business to get any bigger than it already is, because then he's got regulations—he's afraid that he'd haffta hire minorities or something. He's a real prejudiced person—like I said, I would like to have his money—and maybe his attitude of how he keeps money. But in anything else, I would much rather be different from him.

Douglas Giscard's father also achieved moderate financial success in his career as a retail store manager. Mr. Giscard grew up in poverty, the youngest son of a large farming family in Quebec. Douglas realized that his father had worked hard to attain his present status; and while Douglas criticized him for being narrow-minded, too rigid, and too "careful to always be just like society expects him to be," he also admired his father's enterprise and common sense.

Though they faced the full-time job market earlier and with less education than most young men, Sven, Todd, and Douglas each had the advantage of observing their fathers' careers and of garnering insights and information from their fathers' employment experiences. Other young men in the group were not as fortunate. Bobby Jones, Adam Sledge, Harold Thomas, and Jack Thrush all went through adolescence in female-headed households that were wholly or partially dependent on welfare, and these young men had no close, sustained contact with a productively employed adult male. While they observed the financial struggles and employment problems faced by their mothers or older sisters, and felt that they suffered from a lack of models or practical knowledge that could be used to establish productive working lives of their own, they generally believed that, as men, their chances for successful employment were better.

Harold Thomas identified with his older sister, who assumed responsibility for her younger siblings when their parents died. He was discouraged by the hardships the family had experienced and felt it was his responsibility to lighten his sister's load:

> My older sister—she's really had it hard. She's tried her best to take care of my little sisters and brother, and she's really given her heart. I feel closest to her. She can't really make it alone, and I do everything I can for her. Times have been bad. But I hope to make things better if I can. I'd like to see my brother and sisters in a place they can call theirs. That's why I plan to go into the army—so I can do something to help my sister, so I can give 'em more.

Adam Sledge told me that he feels closest to his mother, who has struggled to raise eight children on a below poverty-level income. But he has always been told that he is the "spittin' image" of his father, a man who was chronically unemployed and eventually abandoned the family. Adam dismisses the negative implications of this identification.

> Yeah, I'm good-lookin' too! I may *look* like my father, and I may *talk* like my father—I hear he was a real good talker—but I like to *work!* And I *love* money. [laughter] Hell, I already got two jobs, and I'm thinkin' about gettin' a third one. It ain't gonna be for me like it was with him.

For the young women in our group, family experiences had yielded even fewer effective role models regarding employment. Few of the young women had felt close to their fathers, and none of their mothers had managed to establish careers—or even stable working lives. Though both Sandy Bonds and Jean Ansel lived briefly with fathers who were employed, these relationships were marked by emotional struggle and communication failure. Neither of these young women much understood or identified with her father's role as a worker. Among the young women in our group, only Carrie Green was raised primarily by her father, whom she admires for his employment success and personal traits.

Carrie says she would like to be as self-sufficient as her father, but she is not certain that his independent, self-made approach to life will work as well for her:

> My dad's got a good job; he's a line manager at Black Incorporated. He's also pretty active—does lots of different things—like he golfs, and he goes bowling, and he goes away on trips. And another thing is that he's pretty smart in a lot of things. I hope when I get that old, I'm as smart and as together as he is.
>
> I don't know that much about what he does at work and all. He talks about it sometimes, but he's usually pretty busy. But I guess in some ways my dad prepared me pretty good for life. He always told me, you know: "You gotta go out and get a job. You gotta do it yourself, nobody else will do it for you. You gotta sell yourself and be ready to deliver—you can't get it from me." He always said that ambition and how hard you work were more important than how far you went in school.
>
> I've tried to go out there and do it, and I'm still gonna go on tryin'. But it's hard to get on anywhere good if you're underage. It seems like you need to know somebody to get a good job. Maybe it's just different now from how it was when he was startin' out—I don't know.

Most of the young women in our group had much closer ties with their mothers than with their fathers. In more than half the cases, their mothers were either divorced or single parents. The young women who grew up in female-headed households came away from the experience with different perspectives on the role of the single mother. Genetta Burke, whose mother raised seven children, largely on her own, told me: "Right now, I kinda like the idea of living alone with my kids—not with a husband, but on my own." Luanne Clawson, who grew up in similar circumstances, had a different view: "I wouldn't want to be alone. I don't want to get married and then get divorced. I don't want the responsibility of raising children by myself—it's just too hard!"

All of the young women hoped to establish working lives that were more active and productive than those of their mothers. Even the young women who considered their mothers to be successful as parents said that, while they would like to do as well with their families as their mothers had, they would also like to have more contact with the outside world. Young women, such as Luanne, saw themselves as differing from their mothers by having careers as well as successful family lives:

> I wanna be close to my kids like she is—she seems pretty happy,
> you know, doin' what she's doin'. But she stays home mostly, you
> know? I'd like to have a career—along with marriage and kids.
> Maybe when my kids were real young, I'd stay at home, but I
> wanna work too.

Despite the difficulties they had already encountered in their attempts to establish adult working lives, the young people—both male and female—who saw their parents as playing less than successful roles in the working world, did not feel that their experiences in the labor market were likely to mirror those of their parents. Felisa Santana, whose unemployed parents are supporting a large family on welfare payments, thinks her life will be very different from her mother's:

> My mother had a rough life. She didn't get enough education when
> she was young. She was working in bad jobs all her life—first in
> Puerto Rico and then here. My life will be different 'cause I'm
> getting more education. I've already got more education than
> them—than they had. And I know more about what's goin' on. I
> think if I keep working and keep my eyes open, I'll end up with
> better jobs than what they had.

Several of the young people felt they had learned something about life from watching their parents' mistakes. Todd Clinton said:

> Maybe it did prepare me for life, after all. I learned a lot from
> my family experiences. I think I learned enough to be able to

say that I won't make those mistakes that my parents made—
that I'm not going to *be* my parents. That I never *want* to be
them. That I'm going to do what I want to do—what I think is
best. That I'm going to do it to the best of my ability.

Most of the young people expressed in various ways their need for
relationships outside the family with adults they could admire and emulate.
Few were able to reach out directly. But youth program counselors were
sometimes surprised to discover how much the most apparently guarded or
arrogant young people seemed to crave and respond to attention from a
caring adult. Tough exteriors often camouflaged intense needs. Bobby
Jones, who said, "I depend on *myself*. I never fell back on nobody," also
told me that his CETA project director, John Henry, was "interested in me
'specially." Bobby said: "John can't play no favorites here; it wouldn't be
right. But I know he got an eye on me 'specially, 'cause he knows I got the
potential."

When they came to youth employment and training programs, a
fraction of the young people, like Bobby, seemed to be seeking the individual attention and intensive adult guidance that was lacking in their
experience at home or at school. Bobby spoke with some longing about the
discipline and positive reinforcement that he had received from an eighth-
grade basketball coach:

> That was the best time I ever had—playing basketball. I really liked
> that coach. He was a nice person, but he was strict, you know? He
> didn't jump on you all the time, but when he *did* get mad, he was
> *mad*. He was on my back a little, you know? Talkin' to me—tellin'
> me what to do—that helped.
>
> I like for people to be on my back—tellin' me that I can do it.
> You know, my sister never nagged me much, but I kinda like for
> somebody to do that. John does it sometimes, and it's real good for
> me.

But relatively few of the young people were willing to accept the kind
of paternal guidance that Bobby seemed to want. Though they needed
attention and support, most had a stake in maintaining an independent
stance. They were looking for contact with adults who were willing to treat
them as equals, who would be straight with them about their own experiences, and who would help to provide insights concerning ways of
putting together successful lives. Such relationships were comparatively
rare.

After years of juvenile justice proceedings, foster homes, and unpro-
ductive mandatory counseling, Sandy Bonds met an adult who cared
about her and with whom she could communicate. This woman was a

twenty-five-year-old juvenile probation officer, and Sandy marks their relationship as a turning point in her life:

> She was really straight with me. She didn't tell me what to *do*—she just told me the way things *were*—and I really appreciated that. This may seem minor, but she didn't lie. Neither do I. I don't like people who lie—there's really no reason for it—I really can't say exactly *what* it was she did, but she helped me see myself in a new way. She's just a really *good* person. And I could tell she really cared. And it made me want to—made me realize that I *could* put my life together.

The need for adult support and friendship can be so intense that vulnerable young people become easy marks for those who appear to offer unconditional acceptance and aid while seeking to use the relationship for their own ends. Street hustlers, pimps, and sexual adventurers are obvious examples, but adults in teaching and counseling roles sometimes encourage inappropriate attachments and allow young people to create fantasies of them that the reality of their lives cannot sustain. Several of the young people in our group had experiences along these lines.

Jean Ansel formed an unusually close bond with her drug counselor, one of the first adults she met who treated her as an equal. At first Jean was attracted to this friendship by her counselor's apparent self-confidence and strength:

> My drug counselor, Gloria—when she's working, she seems to be a very strong person. And I always wanted that kind of strength for myself—the way she could work out problems and just go ahead with things—I always wanted that. She really seemed to like me, too, and we started seein' each other as friends. She would talk to me a lot. She's about the only one I ever let know everything that I was thinkin'.
>
> But as I got to know her as a friend, you know, on the side, I found out that she was really very messed up. She sounded good, you know? But she was really messed up inside. She told lies about herself. She looked good at work—in her job—but she didn't really know her own life. She couldn't really control what was going on, you know, in her home situation or her social life. She got me to help her out a lot, with her kids and stuff. But then she started puttin' me down—like she always had to be on top or something. And she was real jealous. She didn't want me to see other people or be with anyone else.
>
> It was hard, you know, 'cause I really cared about her. And I think in some ways she needed me. But finally it was really bad, and I had to stop seeing her.

Through their enrollment in youth employment and training programs, a number of the young people gained access to adults who had enough self-knowledge and control over their own lives to be able to respond with openness, generosity, and objectivity to a young person emerging into adulthood. Such role models were found among program counselors, work supervisors, and older coworkers. Like most relationships of substance, these connections were not formed immediately but developed over time; and their impact extended beyond the more formalized learning processes of the classroom or worksite.

Todd Clinton felt that he gained as much through his association with his program counselor at Portland's Southeast youth center as he did through his CETA-subsidized vocational training at a private cosmetology school:

> Robbie Anderson, my counselor, is really a nice guy. At first I didn't really understand him—he's *there* for you, but he's not the kind of person that's just gonna *give* it to you, you know? He asks questions—hard questions that make you think about things. "You play it straight with me, and I'll play it straight with you"—he's *that* kind of person. Knowing Robbie has been one of the best things about bein' in the CETA program, I guess I admire him more than anybody. I wouldn't want to be a counselor or a social worker, but I'd like to be as straight as Robbie—be as honest and know how I'm feeling—and know how to deal with different situations and different people.

Sexual Roles and Future Families

Among our group of young people, family problems and issues were a major preoccupation. Even those who had left their families behind were inclined to think and worry about their family relationships and earlier experiences at home. In their efforts to establish adult lives, family experience seemed to be the dominant force that shaped their concepts of themselves and the world around them. And possible family roles seemed to be a primary consideration in their projections for the future. But just as their feelings about the past were colored by the often painful contrast between their actual experiences and their idealized family images, their hopes and plans for future family life often seemed to be at odds with the reality of their current circumstances and prospects. The majority of the young people envisioned family lives that approximated the idealized images of their childhood: a stable marriage with a loving, supportive mate, two to three children, and a steady income that would provide the family with ease and security.

While many of the young people held vivid images of what their future family lives would be like, their notions of how such goals would be achieved were vague. Sexual attraction, needs, and attachments constituted a compelling force in the lives of most of these young people. Yet this aspect was seldom given overt consideration in their longer-term plans. For these young people, sex was characterized by compulsion, excitement, confusion, and deep uncertainty, and they did not feel comfortable about examining it closely—particularly in the presence of an adult. In many cases they were forming attachments and making sexual choices that would clearly conflict with their other activities and plans.

The dichotomy of action and intention sometimes made it seem as if the young person were leading a dual life. Some of them dealt with this problem by ignoring the discrepancies. Adam Sledge, whose girlfriend, Cindy, bore him a son midway through our interview period, worked two jobs and talked with some urgency about his plans to move out of his mother's house, marry Cindy, and support his new family. But other times he would speak—as if Cindy and the baby didn't exist—about plans to remain at home for several more years, return to school, win a college scholarship, and eventually move to California. Genetta Burke talked about "finding the right man" someday and settling down to married life, but meanwhile, she continued her exclusive relationship with Virgil, the father of her children.

Others in the group, such as Peggy Bromfield, were more sharply aware of the inconsistencies in their actions and plans and were embarrassed and troubled by these discrepancies. Since her divorce at sixteen, Peggy had been faced with the need to create a stable, independent life for herself and her two children. While she had come to believe that achieving this goal depended upon her own initiative, she also fantasized about being "rescued" by a man who would be a perfect husband and provider. During a period in which she was making a considerable effort to improve her employment prospects, she confessed to me that she was considering yielding to her current boyfriend's entreaties to prove her love and solidify their relationship by having a child together and moving with him to southern Oregon.

Not all of the young people were faced with such dramatic choices and conflicting desires. During the interview period Todd Clinton became engaged to a young woman who was also studying at the cosmetology school. The two seemed to share many interests and aspirations and were looking forward to establishing a hair-design business and raising children together. Others, such as Harold Thomas, whose current attentions were absorbed by the needs of his younger sisters and brother, were still looking forward to finding appropriate spouses and good jobs, which would allow them to start families on a stable and economically secure footing.

Only two of the young people in our group said that they did not intend to marry and have children. Both were young women whose parents had divorced when they were children and whose observations and first-hand experience with male-female relationships had been negative. Jean Ansel, who had worked the streets as a prostitute, said she wanted to focus on a career rather than marriage:

> I'm going to have a career. I want work with a good challenge. From what I've seen so far, I don't want to ever get married. If I ever changed my mind, it would be years from now. But I don't think I ever will. Married life can be just too rough!

Sandy Bonds, who had been independent since her early teens, said she was not interested in men at all and was opposed to marriage:

> I just want to be happy. I hope I can make it as a carpenter. I can see myself—sitting on a rocking chair with my cat beside me—and a house I built myself with a fence around it. I'm a feminist—I'm not interested in men—I like women better. I don't believe in marriage. I don't like the idea—it kind of bores me.
>
> I favor choices for other people. If a woman wants to work, let her go to work. If she wants to be a housewife, let her be a house-wife. Most women with any—well, with *anything* are gonna want to work. Men should figure that out when they get married. I mean, if they figure they're gonna get married to have someone watch the kids while they work, then they don't expect that other person wants to work, too, and expand herself—that's almost crazy!

The young men's views of married life tended to be more traditional than those of the young women. While most of the young women said they intended to work outside the home throughout married life—even when their children were young—the young men were generally uncomfortable with the idea of working wives and mothers. Most of the young men said they wanted to support their future families and would prefer that their wives stayed at home. Sven Latoka said flatly: "I don't think it's a good idea for women to work—they should take care of the house and stuff like that." Both Todd Clinton and Douglas Giscard said they could see how a woman might want to have a career—rather than stay at home all the time. But while Todd was willing to share household responsibilities and to accommodate his future wife's career plans, Douglas's view that housework and childcare were a woman's primary responsibilities was more typical of the young men in the group:

Well, if she just wanted to have a *job*—like at an A & W or something like that—I don't think that's necessary at all. If she had a *career,* it might be different. But when children are small, they need to be tended to. She would need to make sure they're tended to—first and foremost. If she could work and be a good mother at the same time and take care of the house, too. If she couldn't, then I really wouldn't want her working.

Most of the young people were still trying on roles. Their family plans were tentative; few will live out their lives exactly as planned. But their aspirations for family life do reflect some basic values and expectations. Most of the young people intend to marry and establish families. A few want to emulate their parents; but the majority hope to have families that are happier, more stable, and more financially secure than those in which they grew up. While there is some disagreement between the young men and young women regarding the roles they intend to play as husbands and wives, both groups agree that economic security is a key to successful family life. Most of the young men and women in our group believe that their own employment status will be critical in determining the quality of their future family lives.

3. Community Life

No Community Here

> A community is a place where everyone works together, where everyone gets along—takes some pride and tries their best to keep things looking good. I don't call *this* much of a community! This is my hometown, but I have nothing I like about it, really. There's not much to do here if you're young, you know. It looks filthy! And the crime. . . . It's no place for little old ladies—or any ladies, I suppose. And people's attitudes. . . . A long time ago, people were friendly around here. Now everybody's running around trying to put one over whenever they can—you know, that's the worst part of it, really.   *Sven Latoka*

Sven was talking about Jamaica Plain, a Boston neighborhood with about forty-five thousand residents. Once a separate community on the outskirts of Boston, the home of European immigrants who lived in neatly painted woodframe houses and worked in its tanneries and breweries, Jamaica Plain has become an urban neighborhood of sharp contrasts. In the north, there is the Bromley-Heath public-housing project, with its predominantly black and Hispanic residents. Then there is the largely Spanish-speaking area around Hyde Park Square. Next is the central business district, surrounded by the homes of the white working-class and a rapidly growing number of young, white professionals. To the south are Jamaica Pond and Moss Hill, enclaves of the well-to-do.

White, working-class families, such as the Latokas, which until the 1970s constituted the large majority of Jamaica Plain's population, lay the blame for increased crime, physical decay, and deteriorating community life on newcomers to the area—particularly the blacks and Puerto Ricans. Sven says: "The Puerto Ricans and the black people are closing in on this place, and they don't care about the community like the rest of us." But Sven's feelings about his community—or, more accurately, the lack of community in his neighborhood—were echoed by the young blacks and Hispanics I interviewed from other Boston neighborhoods.

Felisa Santana, whose mixed Hispanic/Lebanese neighborhood had recently begun to experience the added pressures of an influx of white professionals, said: "There's not no community up here—not really. 'Cause people are mean, and some are prejudiced. There's always fights up here." Bobby Jones, who lives in a public-housing project in Dorchester, where nearly all of the residents are black, also presented a bleak view of life in his community:

> Around here, everything is dirty and busted up—you know, it looks pretty bad. But I lived here a long time, so I guess I'm used to it. But I would haffta say that the worst thing about it here is people not likin' each other. Wherever you go around here, it's just like that. In Boston, racial problems is real bad, and people just don't get along together. In the neighborhoods, you know, seems like it's the same way—even if you're all the same color—it don't make no sense, you know? It really start from the grown people down—what they say goes down to the kids, and so on.

In their descriptions of community life, most of the young people I interviewed in Boston mentioned negative aspects, such as physical decay, lack of community spirit, racism, crime, and violence. The young people from Portland had better opinions of their community. Those, such as Todd Clinton, Douglas Giscard, and Peggy Bromfield, who had grown up in Portland, tended to take for granted the relatively good quality of life in their city. But newcomers, such as Sandy Bonds (who had lived in Baltimore, Phoenix, Albuquerque, Los Angeles, and Seattle before coming to Portland), were impressed by the city's neighborliness and attractive appearance. Sandy expressed her appreciation for Portland enthusiastically:

> Man, this is a neat town! I love it here. Portland is baby soft compared to every other town I've lived in. It's not rowdy; it's not dirty—that's what I like especially. You can walk down the street and—well, there's not a lot of trash, and drunks, and dead dogs, and shit laying all over the place. You see nice clean streets, and no one hassles you.

Another young woman, who had come to Portland from California, said:

> I love the way it's green here all the time. There seems to be a sort of togetherness—friendliness—among the people that live here— much more so than in other places I've lived. Sort of a friendly atmosphere here most of the time; I've noticed that especially, and I really like it.

While experiences with racial conflict and discrimination influenced the views of many of the nonwhite teen-agers I interviewed, the quality of their neighborhoods and the subsequent feelings they developed about community life seemed to be more related to geographic and social setting than to racial status per se. The black and other nonwhite teen-agers I met in Portland and Kalamazoo were aware of racial prejudice, and most had felt its effects in one way or another, but they did not feel the sense of isolation that the young people living in the public-housing projects and ghettos of Boston felt. As a rule, the physical and social circumstances of their lives were far less abject.

Harold Thomas grew up in a rural community on the Delmarva Peninsula, near the Chesapeake Bay. A descendent of black sharecroppers, Harold was no stranger to poverty and racism. But his life on Virginia's sleepy Eastern Shore did not prepare him for conditions he was to find at the Victoria Point housing project or the racism and violence he en-countered in Boston's public schools:

> When my older sister came up here first, she was tellin' me how
> good it was—how good she could make it in the North. So when my
> folks died, we decided to come up here—which was a big mistake.
> It looked all right at first. When I first saw Boston, I was real
> impressed, with all the buildings and parks and monuments. Then I
> seen the projects—all the tracts and stuff—looked like a jail—or a
> prisoner's camp, like in the war.
>
> I found out there was a whole different kind of racism up here—
> and just people hating each other. I never fought before I came
> here. I try to keep to myself, but there's no way you can live
> without fightin' here. I really don't know. I don't associate with
> people much—I just like to be by myself. There's nothin' here that I
> want.

Adam Sledge, who has spent nearly all of his eighteen years in Victoria Point, agrees with Harold that life in the project does not have much to offer. Through his years of residency and his recent work in Victoria Point on the weatherization project and as a nighttime security aide, Adam has become acquainted with most of the people in the housing project, and he has watched its buildings deteriorate and its population dwindle. Adam says that the only time people in Victoria Point really get together is when there is a threat of trouble from the outside:

> The main thing is there's nothin' much to do here—not too much
> for the kids to get into, you know? Not too many people come in
> the project—especially not too many *white* people. Not because it's
> so bad or nothin', but mainly just 'cause it's a *project*. I mean, why
> come here if you don't have to, you know? But that's one thing
> about it: If anybody from the *outside* was to come *in*, then every-
> body sticks together. Sometimes people from in town come into the
> project and cause trouble. When stuff like that comes down, people

here stick together. But otherwise, everybody's fightin' each other—
you know, quarrelin' and yellin' at each other, rippin' stuff off each
other.

Genetta Burke told me that her major reason for moving out of
Victoria Point was to get her children away from the "hassles and fights"
that were part of life in the housing projects. But she found the same
climate of dissension to prevail in the Dorchester neighborhood where she
now lives. Though the neighborhood is mixed, Genetta says she normally
associates only with other blacks. But even these associations are limited,
as Genetta feels she cannot really trust the people around her. And she
wonders if her experience would be different if she were white or lived
elsewhere:

> When I was growin' up—even in the projects—there was some
> white people around. But we never even associated with 'em at all.
> But I'd really like to, you know, *associate* with different kinds of
> people. 'Cause the people around here—I mean if you really look at
> it—they don't know how to get along together. I mean the *girls,*
> especially. I don't associate much with other women, 'cause the
> simple fact is they always out to stab you in the back, you know?
> Like they tryin' to *get* you. Or maybe they're trying to talk to you
> 'cause they like your old man or somethin'.
>   Maybe white people, or people who live in other places, are
> different. Like if you get a friend, maybe it's a real friend and not
> some half-steppin' friend, somebody that'll come into your house,
> you know, smile in your face, and then take somethin' out of your
> house the next minute. I don't *need* people like that around me. But
> those are the only kind of people who seem to be around me. I feel
> trapped, myself, 'cause I can't enjoy people. I can't relax and enjoy
> bein' with 'em. Livin' around people you can't really associate
> with—I can't live like that! I can't just stay to myself, you know?
> Well, I *can,* most the time, 'cause I done it for a long time. But I
> don't enjoy it.

Racial animosity and interneighborhood conflict served to restrict
the geographic boundaries within which the young people from Boston
lived. Though transportation was sometimes a problem, the young people
from Portland and Kalamazoo generally felt free to move about the city in
groups or by themselves; and they tended to view the entire city as their
community. In Boston, community was usually understood to mean one's
immediate neighborhood. Despite a reasonably efficient citywide transportation system, most of the young people I interviewed in Boston limited
the range of their activities to these confines. Nonwhite teenagers were

particularly careful not to venture onto "enemy turf." Apart from occasional excursions to the downtown business area, which was viewed as a sort of free territory, some of these young people rarely left the housing projects or neighborhoods where they lived and worked.

A segment from one of my interviews with Genetta Burke illustrates the considerations that affected her movement through the city:

GB Simmons Street, where I live, it's all blacks—well, mostly black people. But then there's this next street right here, and we can't go on this street. Yeah, we can't go down there at all.

BS Why?

GB Why? [laughter] 'Cause we'd get jumped.

BS So this street next to you is white?

GB Yeah. And they got a lotta racists down there. They got a big park there too. And if you go down to the park, they all hassle you. You'd get jumped, for sure. You might say it's kind of a dividin' line. They live on the next street over. The park's right in the middle, and you can't even go that way.

BS Is that a problem for you? Not being able to take your kids to the park?

GB Well, no. Not *that* park. You know, there's other parks, where we go. But they're like further away from where we live.

BS Apart from your neighborhood and the park, do you feel like there are other places in the city where you can't go? Places where you wouldn't feel safe?

GB Yeah. Yeah, *lots*. Like Charlestown, East Boston—I won't go near it. Every time somebody tries to get me to go to like Charles Street, you know, I think, "Nah, I don't wanna go down there, 'cause I might get jumped!" They say, "Aw, we won't get jumped." But how do you know? I don't take chances.

BS Well, did you ever actually . . .

GB No, I never got jumped. Well, I almost got jumped by some white boys, but then some people came along and they run off. I did get jumped though by black girls—five black girls. But never, you know, by white people.

BS But you feel you have to be pretty careful?

GB Yeah, around our way, you do. The train station, you know, is in *their* area, but you can go there. They don't usually bother the women, black women. But, you know, sometimes they jump the guys. But it's not just them. It's just that, you know, the black people around where I live, they be, um, you know, they'll knock you down, take your pocketbook—stuff like that. So you gotta watch out all the time.

The restricted mobility of the young people living in neighborhoods such as these had an unfortunate impact on the range of their work preparation and employment alternatives. Regular job-openings in their immediate neighborhoods were nearly nonexistent; and most of the teen-agers I spoke with lacked the base of information, contacts, and confidence needed to seek employment in other parts of the city. They tended to rely solely on the subsidized employment and training opportunities provided by local neighborhood agencies or community centers. While the young people from Portland and Kalamazoo dealt with consolidated program agencies that were operated by the city or school district, and were able to provide access to a relatively wide array of subsidized employment and training options, the young people from Boston dealt directly with local project operators whose range of offerings was, as a rule, very limited.

The youth program delivery-system in Boston was undoubtedly set up with the intention of responding to local circumstances and needs. The neighborhood agencies and community centers seemed to be effective in informing teen-agers of employment and training opportunities and in recruiting eligible participants. Working with the project operators in their neighborhoods and housing projects was convenient for the young people and far less intimidating than having to travel to a centralized program facility and risk dealing with strangers. But the system also served to restrict the young people to project jobs (such as weatherization, construction, and maintenance) and to limit the training and supportive services that neighborhood agencies provide. The system in Boston tended not to broaden the social experience of the young program participants nor to increase their exposure to the world outside their neighborhoods and housing projects.

Few of the young people in our group were satisfied with the roles they were able to play in their communities. Though the young people from Portland and Kalamazoo were less socially isolated than those in Boston, they typically did not feel involved in their communities in any positive or productive way. Teen-agers who drop out of school, receive little supervision from their parents, and have trouble finding or keeping jobs are not viewed as assets in most communities.

Most of the young people complained that they had nowhere to go

and nothing to do. Some of them dreamed of achieving th'
wealth that would one day allow them to make dramatic *f*
contributions to the community. Bobby Jones told me: "After ı ι.
of money, I'll come back here and work in the poor sections. I'd likɛ .
build a big school or auditorium and have it named after me." But few of
the young people could envision more realistic or practical ways to con-
tribute to community life.

Feeling few positive ties to their communities, a number of the young
people defined roles for themselves without regard for community interests
or socially acceptable behavior. "I'm a loner; I stick to myself, and I don't
need nobody else," was a typical comment from members of this group.
But most of them were aware that they were, in fact, dependent on society
in a number of ways, particularly in economic ways. Those who relied on
public welfare and other social service programs, either individually or
through their families, sometimes viewed this dependency as a stigma—evidence of their inadequacy. A number of the young people had channeled
considerable energy into illegal ventures such as shoplifting, drug-dealing,
burglary, prostitution, or other activities that imply a rejection of conventional values. Some of the teen-agers had attempted to retreat from
their personal, social, and economic problems by turning to alcohol
or drugs.

What is life like for a teen-aged criminal offender, alcoholic, or drug
addict? How do young people deal with the obstacles these experiences
present in their efforts to establish viable lives? What is life like for a young
welfare mother? How do teen-agers outside the mainstream view welfare
dependency? In the remainder of this chapter, we will consider the young
people's views and their experiences in these areas.

Alcohol and Drugs

Experimentation with alcohol has long been a rite of passage for
adolescents. But evidence gathered over the past decade suggests that
today's teen-agers are starting younger and drinking harder than preceding
generations. An estimated one in twenty teen-agers has a serious drinking
problem. Among our group of young people, alcohol was by far the most
commonly used drug. Most had taken their first drink by the time they
entered their teens, and several had become social drinkers by age twelve
or thirteen. While most of the young people said they confined their
drinking to weekends or social occasions, several had experienced the
debilitating effects of daily alcohol abuse.

Those who had been dependent on alcohol were inclined to view drinking as a serious problem; but most of the young people did not consider their patterns of alcohol use to be destructive or potentially dangerous and felt that alcohol abuse was a problem for only a small minority of teen-agers. Though some drank sparingly or only on special occasions and others seemed to use alcohol more regularly and sometimes excessively, most of the young people were alike in viewing their own drinking as a harmless and acceptable form of social relaxation. Sven Latoka said:

> My friends and me just usually drink on special occasions—week-ends, usually, I don't know too many people who drink every day. Just mainly on weekends—Friday, Saturday night—we'll go to a movie or somewhere else and drink. Sometimes it gets a little wild. But usually we're just having fun and we don't bother anybody else. I don't see anything wrong with it—having a drink once in a while—how can it harm you?

But several of the young people had witnessed the debilitating effects of alcohol abuse on the part of their parents or other family members, and they maintained that it affected their own drinking practices. Todd Clinton said:

> I like to drink sometimes; but I don't like to get high all that much, and I never get drunk. Alcohol played a big role in my family life. I don't know for sure if my dad is an alcoholic, but he's the kind of person that when he drinks, he drinks to get drunk. When I was younger, he drank a lot. When he was real uptight about something, he'd come home drunk, get real loud, pick fights, and stuff like that. That's one of the reasons we don't get along today. I don't like to be around him when he's drinking. My own attitude is that I said to myself, when I was younger and first started drinking, that if I ever got that way, I'd just quit. I'd never get that way!

As an "illegal substance," marijuana was generally viewed as a slightly more risky and less acceptable drug than alcohol. However, the young people reported that marijuana was readily available to teen-agers in their neighborhoods; it was relatively inexpensive—at least in small quantities—and little stigma was attached to its use. Most of them had tried marijuana at least once, but less than half had become regular users. Some, like Sven Latoka and Carrie Green, found it did not do much for them and said they preferred drinking. Others enjoyed it, but found that frequent use slowed them down too much and interfered with other things that they wanted to to. A number of the young people had been able to make money by selling marijuana on an occasional or regular basis. But at least two of the "dealers," Bobby Jones and Douglas Giscard, said they were not fond of the drug or its effects. Bobby told me:

> Me and my friends don't smoke no more, 'cause, you know, why waste our time? It ain't nothin' but bein' high a little while. Then it just wears off. You spent your money and you ain't got nothin'.
>
> A lotta the older people out this way—the adults, you know —they smoke a lotta weed. And I can see its effects. They forget a lot. They just lay around, and after a while they get real fat—'cause it makes 'em eat. People who are smokin' it all the time just get lazy and don't care about nothin' too much. They lay around and don't get any exercise. That's not for me. I like to move around, keep my body in good shape so I can play ball, you know?

There were others in our group who used marijuana on a regular basis—often in combination with alcohol. Carmeletta DeVries said:

> I don't mess with drugs—no pills or nothin' like that. Usually I just drink a beer and smoke a joint. It's a good way to relax. There's really nothin' wrong with that.

Like Carmeletta, the others who smoke marijuana regularly were inclined to draw sharp distinctions between the relatively mild effects of marijuana and those of stronger or addictive narcotic substances. Genetta Burke pointed out that many of the people she knows smoke "weed" frequently and are still able to work and manage their lives. She said that people who take "coke, pills, or heroin" usually act strange and, because those drugs are more expensive, they are more apt to steal. The young people who smoked marijuana regularly said that it helps them to relax, and they tended to use it more on a therapeutic than a social basis. Harold Thomas told me:

> Since I come up to Boston, I been smoking herb quite a bit. It helps me out a little bit—helps me feel better. I don't see no harm in it. You can get addicted to heroin, but you can't get addicted to marijuana.

While it is well known that traffic in illegal drugs is not confined to urban ghettos and low-income neighborhoods, young people in these settings are generally thought to be at a much higher risk of developing serious drug problems. Drugs of all types are readily available to young people who live in public-housing projects and the poor sections of the inner city, where the circumstances of life seem to encourage the widespread and casual use of narcotics. The young people I interviewed in housing projects and poor neighborhoods were familiar with a wider range of drugs than those who grew up in more middle-class or conventional neighborhoods.

They had the opportunity to observe openly the rituals and effects associated with the use of illegal drugs and they were more candid than other teen-agers about their own use of drugs. But, at the same time, they knew more about the effects of different drugs, were more aware of the dangers of addiction and the often tragic results of drug abuse. They were used to watching out for "junkies," who, as Luana Clawson said, "would do anything for money—hold up, jump, rob, shoot, kill—anything to keep 'em goin' on it." Some of these young people had seen friends, neighbors, and relatives become hooked and eventually die from heroin overdoses. Several, such as Adam Sledge, were actively involved in campaigns to stamp out drug abuse in their housing projects or neighborhoods. Adam said:

> You know, I grew up with some dudes out here who went off into that whole scene. They start shootin' up, you know, and pretty soon they was just *gone.* And I was by myself—you know, that just wasn't what I wanted to get into. If you're messin' with heroin, it don't take long—you gonna start gettin' sick, and you gonna start needin' it. You mess with heroin, and you're on the way out!
>
> I seen it go on in front of my face, and I don't like it. I know a lot of names—but, you know, when it start comin' over to *my* family and friends, somethin's gotta be done. I be tryin' to do somethin' *now.* I work over here for the project security force, you know? We try to tell the people what's happenin'—tell 'em that's not the way to be doin' things out here. 'Cause if they're goin' down, they take me with 'em!

Three young people in our group had been alcoholics and one survived heroin addiction as well. These young people did not grow up in ghettos, they came from white, middle- or working-class families. All three are female. Why did they turn to alcohol or drugs? How did they become dependent? And what effects did their dependencies have on their lives?

Jean Ansel believes that she started taking barbiturates when she was twelve primarily to get attention from her parents. The "downers" did not get Jean the attention or affection she craved, but they did make her high and help her to forget her troubles. Within two years, Jean had "graduated" to heroin—which was much more effective in obliterating her feelings of pain and inadequacy:

> I started takin' downers because of the high. And then I started realizing that when I took 'em, I wasn't ever having to face my problems. I didn't really have to face life at all when I was high. I kept taking 'em for that reason. Then I found out about heroin. I knew this girl, Penny, who was a junkie. She was a few years older than me. She told me about heroin—that it was a whole new life. So I tried it. And I realized that it was a much better life.

It didn't take me long to get hooked. This girl, Penny, lived with her father—he was a lawyer or something—and she was able to write checks on his account. I would come up with about one-fourth or something of what it cost, and she'd pay the rest. Sometimes we stole money from people's purses and stuff. I didn't like that part. But I liked being high!

I liked it because I could stand up and look at everything and everyone and just not care at all. It didn't bother me one bit what happened! I was free. Nothing bothered me. When I didn't get it, I was really bad—bitchy and real upset. Like if I was starting to hurt for it, I'd start, you know, going nuts and all. But when I was on it—you couldn't hardly beat this person!

When she left her father's home and was placed with a foster family, Jean was cut off from her drug supplier. Although withdrawal was painful Jean was able to beat her heroin addiction and live a drug-free life during her seven months in the foster home. But when she moved back to her father's house, she found she still needed a crutch. This time it was alcohol:

I started drinking heavy when I moved back with my dad. I didn't want to get back into drugs, and he and his girlfriend drank a lot, so it seemed okay. From then on—even after I left there—I just kept drinking. I was trying to stay away from drugs as much as I could, you know. I kept thinking that drinking was okay, but drugs wasn't. But then I had a drinking problem.

It took me a long time to realize I was addicted to alcohol. I was on the street then, and everyone I knew drank a lot or took drugs. I finally went to a treatment center. That helped some. I was so disgusted with my whole way of life. I felt if I could quit drinking, it would be a way to get out of it. My job and going to school have helped a lot; I mean, my life now is a lot better and everything. But the only treatment for it, as far as I can see, is just to stay away from it altogether. 'Cause if I drink now, I still want to get drunk!

Though she rarely drinks now, Jean feels that the alcoholism she substituted for her earlier heroin addiction is still a hazard. She fell into a pattern of heavy drinking without realizing that alcohol could be addictive. Another of the young women in our group, Peggy Bromfield, had also slipped into alcohol dependency with little understanding of the potential for addiction.

Peggy started drinking to fight loneliness and ease the discomfort of launching a new social life after her divorce at age sixteen. She had little previous experience with drugs or alcohol when she fell in with a crowd of hard drinkers. She was drinking heavily for over six months before she realized that she had a problem:

Since last December I've been enjoyin' life more. But until then, from February to September, I was an alcoholic. And I don't remember where the time went, really. It was like I had a constant hangover, and I was in a bad mood all the time.

When I left my husband I was like an, um, immature person, just comin' out into the world. You know, it's really kinda hard to get used to bein' single and goin' out with other guys. That was the hardest part—tryin' to figger out which ones were weird and which weren't. You don't even realize when you first get into it, you know? You just have a craving for people and attention, so you want to have people come over and party constantly. I got to know people like that, and like I couldn't leave the kids, you know, so I'd tell 'em to come over and bring their friends over. Everybody's always drinking, so you drink too, you know? There were people here night and day, and I was drinking night and day. Nobody knew it but me, 'cause there were always different people. I'd drink at least a bottle or two of wine every day, you know, and it just never phased me. People would talk about alcoholics and how they get like that, and I finally realized that I could be one. I got to where I couldn't get up in the mornings, and nobody knew what I was drinkin' but me.

I finally decided that I needed to get away from the whole scene—to think about it and what it was doin' to my kids. I went with my grandparents to the beach for a week. They didn't know how I'd been drinkin'. By the second day, I was real shaky, you know, and I wanted a drink real bad. I drank a lot of tea, and that helped some. At the end of the week, I felt a lot better. And I knew I couldn't go back to drinking like I had been.

It's been four months since then, and I feel better all the time. I've only drunk once or twice since then. Now, what I do is smoke a couple hits of hash, and I'm just out. That's not the best thing, I realize, but at least smokin' something that good keeps me from drinking!

The practice of alternating between alcohol and other drugs, or substituting one kind of dependency for another, believed to be less harmful, seems to be a common pattern. Alcohol often seems to be the drug of first choice among young people who have experimented widely with intoxicating substances. Though the use of hashish, marijuana, and even barbiturates was not uncommon, "psychedelic" drugs such as LSD and peyote, were rarely perferred by the several dozen heavy drug-users whom I interviewed. These young people seemed more interested in blunting their sensibilities than they were in "tripping." Alcohol is the most readily available and socially acceptable drug for the very young. Unfortunately, it often proves to be one of the most addictive.

Sandy Bonds took her first drink when she was eleven years old. Her mother, who never drank much herself, kept a bottle of vodka in the kitchen, and Sandy decided to try some. "I took a swig of it and about gagged myself to death," Sandy laughs. "So then I decided to put a little orange juice in it, and it wasn't half bad." Sandy and her friends experimented with drugs and alcohol. She sold drugs and had access to many different kinds. But she returned to drinking, and she acknowledges that it has been a serious problem for her:

> Drugs were a way of hustling, of making money. And they were sort of experimental. I would try this and try that just to see what would happen—just to see how I felt. And because I felt so *bad* then, I would take 'em to make myself feel better. I tried almost everything you could think of, except heroin—I never shot up.
>
> But alcohol was the *main* thing—'cause it's legal. I mean grownups were drinkin' and everything, so it seemed like it would be okay. But it's not. I don't care what anybody says—it's *not*. When you want to drink to escape or when you drink and you're an alcoholic, it's not okay. I don't even understand why they even got it legal—except for the fact the government makes so much money off it.
>
> Alcohol is kind of a "get-away" type thing. Everybody says that alcohol is something just to ease the mind, relax, or just a social thing. That's not what it is. Alcohol is a real *escape* for a lot of people 'cause it *works*. It's a depressant, but it sort of—well, it almost turns into an upper when you're depressed and you drink it. I don't know *how* that works. Umm—I kind of wish they never even had the stuff around. But I *do* like it. I *still* like it, and I *still* drink it. I don't drink to where it's going to hurt me anymore. Umm—that's what I learned from drinking. I mean, I know when it's going to hurt me, and when it's not. So I can regulate myself on that. Mostly I don't drink at all. And when I do drink, I know that I'm drinking to get drunk.

Crime

High crime rates, particularly in the major urban centers of the country, are a symptom of dysfunctional community life. Though criminal activities are obviously not confined to the young, youths are both the victims and the perpetrators of a substantial portion of the crimes that take place in our cities. About one-quarter of all persons arrested each year are under eighteen years old, and another 30 percent are between eighteen and twenty-two.

Teenagers who are out of school and unable to find work are among those most likely to become involved in crime. Illegal activities can provide them with the income they need to survive or allow them to obtain things they would otherwise have to do without. Those who lack positive and rewarding roles at home, at school, at work, or in the community may feel they have little to lose by engaging in criminal acts.

Among our group, nearly all of the young people reported that they had been involved in some kind of illegal activity. While some had been apprehended only for status offenses, such as possession of alcohol or tobacco, curfew violation, truancy, running away from home, or other actions that would not be considered crimes if committed by adults, about half had engaged in more serious offenses, and a number had accrued substantial police records.

Next to illegal drug use, shoplifting was the crime most frequently committed by the young people in our group. All but two (Luanne Clawson and Tien Van Chin) admitted they had stolen something from a store at one time or another. Some of the young people, such as Sven Latoka, Todd Clinton, and Peggy Bromfield, said their shoplifting had been limited to a few experimental ventures in early adolescence. All three had been caught shoplifting by store personnel; and though the punishment was usually not severe, these young people felt the experience of getting caught was a major deterrent. Sven said:

> My friends and I got into stealing cigarettes at the drug store—until this one time when I got caught. I was about twelve at the time. I knew the people in the store, so it was real embarrassing. They give me a lecture, and they called up my parents. My dad had to come down and get me. He give me a lickin' when we got home—you can bet I never did *that* again.

A number of the young people had been habitual shoplifters; and while they claimed to have stopped this practice, they also indicated that they did not think it was "all that big a deal." Carmeletta DeVries said, "I never did anything *bad,* you know—just shopliftin' is all." She went on to explain that stealing from a store is much different than stealing from another person, because "stores expect a certain amount of it [stealing], and they can cover it with no problem." Adam Sledge, who had been caught stealing a transistor radio from a department store, said: "It wasn't nothin' serious, you know—just shopliftin'—but it was my second offense, so I got put on probation."

Among the young people that I talked to, females were much more likely than males to have engaged in habitual shoplifting; clothing and cosmetics were the things they were most likely to have stolen. "Looking good" seemed to be considered particularly important among the young black and Hispanic women from the housing projects and inner-city neighborhoods. Several young women told me they would rather stay home than go out anywhere if they did not have anything "nice" to wear. Felisa Santana, who seemed always to be stylishly dressed, said that she got many of her clothes from a younger sister, who was "one of the best shoplifters in the neighborhood."

Luanne Clawson, who said she had never stolen anything herself, offered the following, rather confused but revealing, comments on the differences between the criminal activities of "girls" and "boys" and the motivations involved in theft:

> The girls don't really steal that much—only if they're out shopliftin', right? That's probably all. But if you hear of somebody rob a house, a bank, or shoot somebody, you know, that's gonna be a boy. The girls, you know, shoplift. All they do is shoplift clothes and stuff—'cause they *need* 'em.
>
> Me, myself, I never did anything like that. I think it's bad—even if you want something real bad, you know? But the boys—like Bobby Jones, you know? All right, now if *he* seen somethin' that he wanted real bad, you know, and he didn't have the money or nothin' for it, he has no choice but to take it—if he really wants it, right? All right, but now if I was in Bobby's shoes, you know—since he works and he got a job now—well, if he just put a little money aside each time, out of each check, then he could save up and get whatever he want. It's wrong to steal somethin' from another person or to hurt somebody to get what you want. But some people just don't look on it that way. They just thinkin' about what *they* need and what *they* want.

Most criminal offenses committed by teen-agers—male or female —are property offenses rather than crimes of violence. While young men are more than four times as likely as young women to be arrested for nonstatus offenses, about 90 percent of all arrests in the under-eighteen-year-old population are for nonviolent property crimes. Bobby Jones, the young man who was cited as a negative example by his classmate, Luanne Clawson, was one of the few teen-agers I interviewed who had been convicted of a violent crime.

Bobby was fifteen when he first got involved in illegal activities. He told me that he used to "run errands—carry stuff for the players in the project" as a way of making money. He also stole marijuana from apartments in the project and sold it to other teen-agers. He and his friends would hot-wire cars that were left unattended, ride around in them for a few hours, and then abandon them. Though he admitted to occasional purse-snatching during this period, Bobby says he did not hurt people. But when he was sixteen, and had been unemployed and out of school for about six months, Bobby was arrested for unarmed robbery and sexual assault. Along with four other young men, he had stolen some food stamps from a young woman in the project. She was carrying them in her pocket when the boys "jumped her."

Bobby claims there was really no sexual assault and says he was surprised that the young woman, who was an acquaintance, actually pressed charges:

> Me and the four other dudes, we messed with the girl—just played with her is all, really. When she called the cops on us, we didn't believe it, you know? 'Cause we knew her and everything. We couldn't believe she was serious.

Following their arrest, Bobby and his friends were kept in juvenile detention for four days. Bobby's sister posted the $5,000 bail and appeared with him in juvenile court at the sentencing. Bobby says two of his friends, who already were on probation, were "sent away," but as a "first-timer," he got off light. Bobby was put on probation and ordered to pay a $125 court fee. He used money that he "earned" through illegal drug sales to pay his fine; but he did not report to his juvenile probation officer, and he was never contacted by the court after his sentencing.

Though he maintains that he was more careful after this experience, Bobby continued his criminal involvements. He experienced no serious repercussions from his first brush with the law; but the second time he was caught, the results were more impressive:

> After that first time, you know, I didn't do too much. I still used to ride around in stolen cars sometimes. I didn't steal 'em myself, but I still used to fool around in 'em. And I stole other things—smaller stuff—a couple of times. But then, you know, somethin' happened to me, and it got me to realizin' what can happen if you really get caught. I can't see myself in no jail, you know. That first time I told you about, here in Boston, that was just *boring*. We played pool there, watched TV, eat, got to sleep. It was an experience—that was all. But there was another time I got caught, and *that* time was much worse.
>
> This happened after I first got workin' on the CETA project, not too long ago. I went to Baltimore for the weekend with a friend of mine. Me and my cousin, who lives in Baltimore, and his friend, and their two girlfriends, we was riding around in a stolen car. My friend went off someplace to go see somebody he knew. And we got caught—*I* got caught; he didn't.

I had to stay down there—on account of this big blizzard they was havin' in Baltimore. It started snowin' when we first got down there, and it was really goin' by the time we got caught. I was put in jail and I had to stay there. First I was in their police station there—it's just like a jail, you know? I was in sentry there from Sunday night 'til Wednesday afternoon. Then they put us over in the city jail, until my people, my aunt and my grandmother, come in Friday and got me out. They might've got me out earlier, but the blizzard. . . .

This city jail is ten blocks wide—like a penitentiary or somethin'! I was in jail with grown men—hoods, faggots, *everything*. You should see it! It was a trip. They had men in there that looked just like women! That experience, after that, made me realize that I couldn't do no more crime. I was lucky nothin' happened to me. If anyone would've tried somethin', they would've had to kill me to do it. But I met some dudes from the jail house that got transferred over with me. We stayed together, and nobody really tried nothin'. But there was dudes in there who were pimpin' the faggots for five dollars and stuff like that. I was real scared the whole time I was there. 'Cause it's big—*real* big—and there's no tellin' what could happen to you.

I was real lucky I got let go. They didn't have a record on me of any trouble in Boston, so they thought it was a first time. Instead of givin' me a sentence, they finally just let me go back to Boston. I think I was very lucky, 'cause the judge told me I could've got five years. They're real strict down there. 'Cept for bein' in jail, you know, nothin' real bad happened to me over it. My people, they didn't tell anybody up here what happened. But, you know, it was a *bad* mistake on my part. And after that I realized that I couldn't do nothin' else like that—'cause the goin' to jail—it was *real* scary.

While Bobby claimed that spending time in a big city jail with adult criminals scared him into going straight, I met other teen-agers who claimed that getting caught and spending a day or two in adult jails or police lock-ups was "no big deal." Sandy Bonds, who was arrested and incarcerated a number of times for relatively minor offenses, claimed it had little effect on her subsequent involvement in illegal activities:

I was busted a lot of times—for selling acid, selling pot, selling pills and things—for drinking too. When I lived in New Mexico, the drinking age was twenty-one. I drank constantly, and I was always gettin' busted for that. Seemed like most every weekend I would get busted and hauled off to jail for somethin'. Then I'd go up before a judge, and he'd spank my hands and say, "Don't do that anymore."

But it didn't do any good, 'cause sooner or later I'd just do it
again.

Sandy's problems with the law continued for a number of years. In
addition to drug-dealing, drunkenness, and disorderly conduct, she was
apprehended by the police for her participation in gang fights that were
prevalent within the high school she had been attending in New Mexico.
Sandy was identified as one of the chief troublemakers, expelled from
school, and remanded to a juvenile detention home by the court. The
counseling that Sandy received at the detention home was continued for a
number of months after she was put on probation, and it proved to be
more effective than her earlier jail experiences in changing her attitudes
about herself and her propensity for getting in trouble:

> I got this really good P.O. officer, Susan Fisher, that I told you
> about before. And I had to go to a treatment facility. The whole
> time I went there I was in a kind of psychotherapy type thing.
> There were a couple different psychiatrists I would talk to. They
> had established me as "emotionally unstable"—which was kinda
> weird—but the whole experience was good for me. My P.O. officer
> was the best, but everybody told me I was better than what I had
> been acting like—that was the main thing. I got it pumped into my
> head: "You're not a bad kid," and "Show yourself what you can
> do!"
>   At the time, I didn't understand everything that was happening.
> But it turned out to be a really good thing for me, and I'm glad they
> did it. Because, if they hadn't, I wouldn't of been able to sit here
> and talk to you like this. I wouldn't be working, like I am now. I've
> got more self-respect now, and you need to have that to do almost
> anything. I mean, how can you make a decision about yourself if
> you don't know yourself and you don't respect yourself? How can
> you make a *good* decision? It's almost impossible. You've got to
> know something about yourself—respect yourself—before you can
> make any good decisions.

Most of the young people I interviewed who had been in serious
trouble with the law seemed to have little understanding of their own behavior. Their participation in crime was spontaneous and involved little
forethought. In some cases, the illegal activities they described seemed to
be random and almost senseless. Other times they were obviously so absorbed, as Luanne Clawson put it, with what *they* needed and what
they wanted at the moment, that they did not think or care about the
effects that their actions had on others—or even on themselves. I met
several young people, though, who planned their criminal acts with considerable deliberation and who felt morally justified in committing them.

Douglas Giscard began a two-year burglary career by robbing donation boxes in Catholic churches. Given his history of conflict with strait-laced parents and parochial school officials, it seemed to him to be poetic justice:

> It was an easy way to make money, and I really felt justified in
> doing it. We used to pick out a church almost every weekend. They
> had little poor boxes, and they'd put bills through the little slots.
> We'd go in the back and put our combs down there, catch the bills
> in the teeth, and pull 'em up. There were always wealthy people
> that would come to church and put tens and twenties in there every
> so often. We'd keep an eye out for stuff like that. I figured we were
> poor, after all, so they might as well give it to us.

Douglas was living with his friend, Gil, when they began burglarizing houses. Douglas is an intelligent, methodical, and not particularly aggressive young man. He says that he never wanted to hurt anyone; but he needed money, and burglary seemed a logical, fairly safe way to go about getting it. He learned the techniques of a burglar in much the same way that young people learn more conventional skills:

> How did I figure it out? Well, I watched people. I knew it was going
> on, you know, ever since I was a child. Our house had been bur-
> glarized and I was real curious at the time. I learned a few tricks
> from older friends on how to do it the fastest and easiest ways.
> There's really no stopping burglars once they know what they're
> doing—it's hard to catch 'em.

Douglas's burglary career came to an abrupt halt when he was arrested. "There was no question that I was guilty," he admitted, "I was caught red-handed in the process. And I think I was handled reasonably and fairly by the police." Douglas had a preliminary hearing in juvenile court at which he pleaded guilty. He was released on his own recognizance and later placed on probation. Douglas knows he got off easy because he had no previous arrests. He was nearly eighteen years old and could have been remanded to an adult court, where the penalty would likely have been much stiffer.

The caseworker assigned to Douglas by the court told him that he would have to find a job or return to his parents' house. Douglas was able to get work as a dishwasher, but he found the job boring and quit after several months. Douglas said he was not opposed to working in a "straight" job, and he realized that he could not expect to make the kind of money he had been making as a burglar; but he did not want a job that was "stupid and boring," and he wanted to feel that he was getting somewhere through his work. His caseworker referred Douglas to Portland's Southeast youth center for CETA placement. But finding the right kind of placement for someone like Douglas was not easy. As his CETA counselor said: "He's a smart kid, and he's made good money. Anything we find for him is going to pay minimum wage. So it's not the money that's going to motivate him; he needs a challenge—something he can get his teeth into."

Welfare Dependency

Within our group of young people, most had experienced some sort of dependency on welfare or other income support programs before they became involved in CETA-subsidized employment and training activities. More than half came from families whose reliance on AFDC, state-funded welfare, or supplemental social security payments had extended over a number of years. About a third of the teen-agers had applied for and received some kind of income support—either as individuals or as heads of their own households. Only four of the sixteen had no firsthand experience as welfare recipients. How do the young people in our group view welfare dependency? And how are their attitudes affected by their own experience, or lack of experience, with the welfare system?

Negative views of the welfare system and those who relied on it for support seemed to be prevalent among the young people I met from non-welfare-receiving families—particularly in the white working class. As they were growing up, these young people had heard their parents, neighbors, and other adults complain about "welfare bums" and people who did not want to work but did not mind living off the labor of others. Sven Latoka told me: "People get on it [welfare] 'cause it's easier than going out and finding a job. Once they're on it, they just get lazy and stay on the dole all their lives."

While most of these young people seemed to feel that the availability of welfare encouraged laziness and dependency, some were willing to acknowledge that welfare could help people whose needs were genuine. "Welfare's gotten a bad name," observed Todd Clinton, "There's people around who are just out to take what they can get. But there's others who *can't* work; and if it weren't for welfare, they wouldn't be able to live."

I expected that young people who had grown up in households that depended upon welfare support would have views on welfare recipiency that differed substantially from those with no firsthand experience. I found the young people I interviewed from welfare-dependent families to be more knowledgeable about the system, and their criticism was typically more intense and specific. A number of them pointed out that while the benefits provided by welfare were not really adequate, the system discouraged recipients from earning additional money through employment. Bobby Jones said:

> It's no good livin' on welfare. You don't get too much, you know? They say, if you on welfare, you not supposed to have a job. How they think you gonna get by? If you do find a job—which most people do, sooner or later—then they cut you down—only give you so much. I think people should be allowed to get their welfare checks and work too. Everything's goin' up, you know? People havin' like four or five kids, they may get somethin' like only two, three hundred dollars from welfare. They need more. They need to work, but they can't afford to give up the welfare.

The young people from welfare-dependent families generally were aware that recipients are often viewed with hostility by those who tax dollars support the system. Some were defensive about their family's welfare status, but many believed that the system *was* open to abuse by people who did not want to work and were willing to take advantage of others. Felisa Santana, whose parents had been on and off welfare a number of times, said: "Some people do take it just to stay home and be lazy. They don't have to get on it, but they do. Other people need it, and they won't give it to them." And many of these young people seemed to agree that reliance on the welfare system discouraged initiative and fostered unhealthy dependency. None of them wanted to be welfare recipients when they "grew up." Most of them had views of chronically welfare-dependent people that were as negative as those prevalent among the young people whose families had never relied on welfare. Adam Sledge said:

> The way it seems to me, I just rather do somethin' for myself. I don't want nobody to give me too much of anything. I guess some people say they like welfare, and lots of other people don't. To me, I don't think it's no good at all. 'Cause it keep people from learnin' to do things they need to do or want to get into. Those people on it, they get lazy. They just sit around and get free things. That shouldn't be. They should be out tryin' to do something on their own.

Luanne Clawson, who had been raised by her mother on AFDC, maintained that she would never apply for welfare herself, because "it's better to work, and they don't give you that much to bother with anyway." She felt that fathers who failed to support their children were the major cause of welfare dependency, and she also found fault with older children who failed to help their mothers or to assume responsibility for themselves:

For some people—especially those that has a lot of kids—I know it's real hard. So many kids won't get out there and get themselves a job. But, you know, it's really the father's department—'cause he shouldn't go around givin' people babies, if he's not gonna see about 'em after. That's why families have to get on welfare—it's the fathers—they just up and leave you and don't give the kids no support or nothin'. I think that's wrong.

My mother's on welfare, and me and my older sister, we help her out. She's doin' better nowadays, 'cause she only has one kid more to take care of—that's my little sister, that's nine. The rest of us, you know, we're more on our own. We help out. We know what's happenin' out here.

Some of the young people believed that welfare dependency and abuse had become such serious problems that the entire system was in jeopardy. Harold Thomas felt that welfare probably should be abolished, but he worried about what would happen to those who had come to depend upon it:

I don't like it. I mean, everybody should be gettin' a job and not dependin' on the government for support. Welfare needs to go away, anyway, and everybody needs to be working. I don't really think welfare is gonna be around too much longer. And while people are just sittin' home doin' nothin', it's just gonna slowly disappear. And it's gonna end up bein' more difficult for them that's been on it to get a job.

While welfare dependency was viewed as a major problem by many of the young people, there were others who saw welfare and other income-support programs as a temporary safety net or a lift on the road to economic self-sufficiency. These young people felt that the usefulness of such programs outweighed any potential for abuse. Jack Thrush, from Kalamazoo, said that while he hoped he would never need to apply for welfare, he could envision circumstances under which it might become necessary for him to do so. But he also said, "I'd be lookin' for a job all the time, working to get off it, you know? That's what my mother did when she was on it." Tien Van Chin spoke favorably of programs that provided young refugees with temporary income support. Because of such support, several of his friends had been able to finish school and find better-paying jobs. Both Jean Ansel and Douglas Giscard said they were grateful for the support they had received from an independent-living subsidy program, sponsored by the City of Portland. Both left the program when they were able to obtain CETA jobs. Douglas said:

They provide a juvenile with a way to go, when he's in a position that he can't really hack it on his own yet. They give you about $310 a month to pay for an apartment, bills, food, and other stuff. It's set up so that you work. You find a job, and whatever you make is subtracted, and they pay the difference. They help you to make a budget and all. I was on it for about three months—until I was able to leave it, and stand on my own two feet. It was a stepping-stone on the way up—a very helpful thing for me.

Within our group were several young people who thought of welfare as temporary or emergency support when they first applied, but found themselves still depending on it after several years' time. Young women who were single parents found it especially difficult to avoid or escape welfare dependency.

Peggy Bromfield first got on AFDC when she was pregnant and her husband was unemployed. Her dependency continued after she was divorced. Like many of the other young welfare mothers I met—particularly those who had come from middle-class families—she was keenly aware of the social stigma of welfare dependency and dissatisfied with her own reliance on AFDC:

> I always suspected that my husband lost his job purposely so that welfare would pay for the pregnancy and the hospital bills. I guess he thought that was a smart investment, but I think it's a cop-out. If I ever have another baby, I'll find some way to pay for it myself.
>
> Socially, there's a lot of negative things about bein' on welfare. People think less of you when they know you get welfare. Even the people in the welfare office look down on you—when, you know, they probably just barely got out of high school themselves and were lucky to get a job. They look down on you, and they show it, and that hurts, you know? It's degrading.
>
> I don't like to tell people I'm on welfare, because I think they'll look down on me. It changes the way people feel about you. But I'm pretty honest, so I usually tell 'em anyway. When someone asks me where I'm comin' from, I have to say, "Welfare." I wish I could lie—I'd tell you a good lie—but I'm not into lying, so now you know the truth."

Among the young mothers who dealt with the welfare office on a regular basis, stories about the inefficiencies, inequities, and absurdities of the welfare system abounded. They complained about frequent changes in procedure, poor communication among staff, and lack of communication with other social service agencies. One young woman in Portland, who needed emergency help with her winter fuel bills, was told by her AFDC caseworker that she qualified for a special program. But she was given the wrong referral information, and she missed several afternoons of work in her CETA program job and was sent to six different agencies before she finally found someone who could assist her. Many of the young mothers had experienced frequent disruptions in their work training activities and household schedules when they were asked to report to the welfare office—often for relatively minor concerns that could have been handled over the telephone.

While several young women said their AFDC caseworkers were helpful and understanding, others felt they were treated by their caseworkers with disregard, suspicion, and hostility. A young mother from Boston said:

> The one |caseworker| I got now, she gives me trouble all the time—all kinds of trouble. She act like I'm tryin' to take somethin' away from *her.* I don't know *what* she thinks, really. She just troubles me for nothin'. I won't be doin' nothin' to her, and she'll just call me up and tell me I gotta go down there for somethin'. But when I get down there, she won't be there, you know? I end up waitin' around for a couple hours. And when she finally get around to me, it's really nothin'—or just some little thing, you know? I pack the kids up and get all ready for trouble and then—nothing!

The meagerness of welfare grants in relation to the cost of living, the penalties for additional earned income, and the administrative barriers that must be navigated to receive support provide both the incentive and rationale for welfare "chiseling." During my interviews I heard a number of stories about women who worked and augmented their AFDC grants with unreported earnings in order to support themselves and their children. But I met only one young woman who was willing to provide firsthand confirmation of this practice and to discuss in detail her own experience as a "welfare cheater."

Genetta Burke had been receiving AFDC payments for over four years—since the first of her two children was born. Genetta says she could never support her family on the AFDC checks alone; and though she does not like to cheat, she feels justified in not reporting her full income.

This practice started shortly after her sixteenth birthday, when Genetta got a temporary job as an office helper. She says that she reported this change in employment to her AFDC caseworker and that he told her "since the job was only gonna last for six weeks, it was better not to hassle with the paperwork and risk losing my welfare over it; and I should just go ahead and do it, and not say anything to the other people in the welfare office." During the next three years Genetta earned money babysitting for friends, and she also put in three short stints as a factory worker. None of the income she earned was reported to the welfare office.

When we met, Genetta was receiving a AFDC grant of $152 every two weeks. She was also bringing home about $85 each week from her job on the weatherization project. The welfare office had been notified about her CETA job, and this income had been the source of some conflict between Genetta and the AFDC staff:

> Oh, they said they was gonna cut me off from welfare, 'cause I was in this program. They was checkin' up on people, you know? They had this computer that checks up on people's earnin's? Yeah, well, my social worker, she tried to interview me about it—told me I could get in some real trouble over it. But we was able to get a waiver or somethin' like that. 'Cause Henry, you know, my supervisor? He called legal aid and got me a lawyer. And after that, when I told her I had a lawyer, she just dropped it. And I was able to keep the money I make here.

Genetta had other sources of income as well. Her grandmother, who lived with Genetta and her children, was contributing about $150 for household expenses from her social security check each month. Genetta's boyfriend, who no longer lives with her but is the father of her children, was also providing money to the household. Genetta said, "He's pretty good about that. He pays for my daughter to go to nursery school—$25 a week. He pays for that regular and gives me a little extra money for food and stuff like that sometimes."

When income and contributions from all sources were totaled, I discovered that Genetta was receiving between $800 and $900 a month to support a family of four. This put the Burke household well above the poverty guidelines set by the federal government, though they still fit within the low-income family category. Genetta had no problem handling basic expenses such as rent, which was $175 a month, or heating oil, which was costing nearly $100 a month during the winter; but after food, clothing, transportation, childcare, and other household necessities are purchased, Genetta reported that there was usually no money left.

Genetta feels that she is just trying to do the best she can for herself and her children. And while she acknowledges that she "makes out pretty well compared to lots of the people around here," Genetta would like to be more self-sufficient:

> I'd like to get off welfare, you know? I like workin', and I'll probably always work. But for now—I mean, just to make what I

need to keep things goin'—I'm not even doin' that good now—but without welfare, I'd need to make at least $5 or $6 an hour. And I just don't think that right now I could get a job that paid much.

Genetta's situation seemed to be far from typical; her monthly income exceeded the earnings of her work crew supervisors at the weatherization project and was much greater than that of most of the other young people I encountered during my research. Making ends meet seemed to be a constant struggle for most of the young welfare mothers that I interviewed. But Genetta's story does illustrate a dilemma common among the minority of young people who have learned to manipulate the welfare system or otherwise maximize the benefits of life on the margins of society. The desire for self-sufficiency, social acceptance, and other rewards that can come from a working life in the mainstream must be weighed against the loss of benefits and the uncertainties of competing at a disadvantage in a new environment.

Given the nature of the welfare system and the attitudes about welfare dependency that prevail in most communities, it is not surprising that most of the young people in our group would much rather work than collect welfare. If anything, those with firsthand experience as recipients are even more eager than nonrecipients to avoid welfare dependency in later life. But for many, particularly for single mothers with small children, welfare dependency is a difficult trap from which to escape. The low-paying, dead-end jobs that are available to teen-agers who are unskilled, uncredentialed, and inexperienced do not really offer a viable alternative to welfare. Whether the young people in our group will be able to achieve and maintain economic self-sufficiency in their adult lives remains to be seen, but there is little doubt that this is what most of them want very much to do.

4. Schooling

Not the Way It Should Be

> When I was in high school, nobody was impressed with me. The teachers were only impressed with certain kinds of people—the jocks, who played all the big sports, the achievement freaks, who got straight As, and the people who more or less did just exactly what the teachers said—and that wasn't me, you know? I just didn't get across the way they wanted. I wasn't outstanding, and I wasn't into brown-nosing. I just didn't let them walk on me—that was all. They didn't seem to want to have much to do with you in high school if you had a mind of your own. That's not the way it *should* be, but that's the way it *was.*   *Todd Clinton*

Todd is not the only one who feels that his high school career was less than successful. Most of the young people in our group think there is a big difference between how school should have been and how it was for them.

Apart from their families, school had been the most important institution in the lives of the teen-agers I interviewed. It gave them their first and most sustained experience with the world outside their homes. In school they began to discover where they stood in relation to others. Though the discoveries often proved to be disconcerting, they were told that their experience in school would provide the base for their future lives. Going to school is what children do, so that they may learn to become adults. And for years, they went—though many of them were bored, uncomfortable, or unhappy with their lives at school. Some of them blamed the system. Some of them blamed themselves. But by the time they reached high school, most of the young people in our group were convinced that they would never fit in and that there was not much use in trying.

The problems they faced in school were varied. Some of them were frustrated in their attempts to develop academic skills and were embarrassed about being slow learners. Others felt condemned to social obscurity because they lacked the confidence, looks, athletic ability, family background, or other qualities they viewed as prerequisites for recognition or even acceptance in their schools. Some of them found it impossible to get along with their teachers or other students, and they were always getting into trouble. Others never attracted much attention to themselves; they simply put in their time at school and invested as little as possible in activities which they viewed as boring and pointless.

While most of the young people acknowledged that the school system was at least intended to provide them with the benefit of an education, there were a number who saw mandatory school attendance as a tool by which society tried to control their lives. They questioned the basic assumptions of an education system that had required them to spend six or seven hours a day, five days a week, thirty-six weeks a year in a classroom, under the charge of teachers in whose selection they had no voice, performing tasks about which they had little choice. Sandy Bonds's comments about her high school experience were typical of this group:

> I hated high school with a passion! There were a lot of things I didn't like—some of the people, some of the teachers, the whole routine—but mostly the fact that it was *mandatory*. That really got to me, you know? The attitude was: "There's nothing you can do about it—you have to go to school and don't give me no shit." That was it, you know? Everybody said you *have* to do it *this* way, and I didn't have a choice to do what I wanted—that really upset me.

Young people with strong needs to make their own decisions and control their own lives are likely to run into trouble in the school system. "I'm not gonna say that I just do whatever I want," Sandy told me, "but it's always been real important to me to do what *I* want and what *I* think, and not what someone else tells me to do." Some young people, such as Sandy, who had received little supervision from their parents and had already developed an independent outlook by early adolescence, did not submit easily to the discipline imposed by school authorities, and they were apt to view school routines, requirements, and rules as a personal affront. Reports from these teen-agers on their high school experiences were crowded with accounts of alleged violations, unjustified punishment, retaliation, showdowns, fights, truancy, and suspensions. I got the impression that their teachers never knew quite what to make of them and probably breathed a sigh of relief at their final exit.

The relief in most cases was mutual—these young people did not really understand the school system, but they were glad to get out of situations that were uncomfortable and seemed perversely unfair. Jack Thrush, whose family experience was in many ways similar to Sandy's, told me:

> School always seemed really weird to me. I wasn't interested in doin' what they wanted me to do, and I didn't like sittin' in class.

So most the time, I'd end up skippin'—just come there to meet my friends and then leave. When I did go to class, I'd usually get in trouble. I had a real hard time talkin' to the teachers—they all seemed so *rigid* or something, you know?

The first time I quit school for awhile, it was 'cause I had got kicked out for ten days. I was busted for grass—even though I wasn't even smokin' it at school—and that blew the rest of the tenth grade. But I went back to school. I decided to go back and try harder in the eleventh grade. And I did pretty good for about the first three days—'til I showed up at my math class.

See, my schedule was messed up, so I had missed two days. I hadn't been there yet, and it was the third day of school. When I got there, the teacher was talkin' to all the students. And I knew right away, when I heard him, it wasn't gonna work. He was supposed to be gettin' to know us and all—tellin' us about the class. And he started sayin' stuff like, "When you're in this class, I want you to forget about all your other classes." He said, "When you're in here, this is the most important thing that's happening. This is the world, and I'm God." I couldn't believe it—he was talkin' like he held all the power in his hands. I couldn't believe that everyone could just sit there and let him go on like that! Then he said somethin' like, "If anybody thinks they're gonna get out of any work in this class, they're gonna have to deal with *me*. If you can't live with that, you better leave now." I raised my hand, and I said, "I'm leavin' now, and I'm *never* comin' back." And I got up and walked out of the school—and I never did go back either.

Douglas Giscard was another strong-minded teen-ager who walked out of school and never went back. When he got into trouble in the public high school he was attending, his parents enrolled him in a strict Catholic school, where "you had to keep your hair really short, have your shirt tucked in all the time, and you couldn't wear tennis shoes." Douglas felt he had little in common with the other students. "I stayed out of the public eye," Douglas told me, "I don't like to associate with people when I'm against their principles." His major confrontations were with the teachers, who, he felt, were inflexible and dictatorial. Douglas said:

> It isn't right to try to control somebody's mind—to insist that they learn just what you'd like them to. High school should be changed. I'd like to change it so that a kid could go into a classroom and study whatever he wanted for as long as he feels like studying. He shouldn't feel pushed into it. He should get what *he* wants to get out of it—not what other people want him to get.

Douglas, Jack, and Sandy were quick learners. Though they were not inclined to study in school and learned little about subjects in which they had no interest, their reading skills were good and they were able to pick up much of what they wanted to know on their own. But there were others in our group who had a much harder time learning basic academic skills.

Though they lagged behind most of their classmates in grammar school and junior high, Carrie Green, Luanne Clawson, and Bobby Jones were able to get through their early years of schooling without much attention being focused on their learning problems. But when they reached high school and were expected to work more independently and study more sophisticated subjects, their failure to master basic skills became a serious problem. Carrie Green described the difficulties she faced in her tenth grade biology class:

> I was never a good student in school, but I managed to get by—
> until I started taking harder classes in the tenth grade—that's when
> I ran into trouble. Biology, especially, was real hard for me. I was
> like a slow learner. The whole class would be working away, and I'd
> just be sitting there, tryin' to figure out what was goin' on. I had
> trouble reading the book, and I couldn't remember things—like the
> terms they used—I just couldn't keep 'em straight. I would try to
> raise my hand, you know, when I didn't understand. But I hated to
> keep interrupting the whole class. I felt like a dummy, and the
> teacher, you know, she wouldn't want to slow everyone down just
> for me.

Carrie did not like to attract attention to herself and her learning problems. She found it embarrassing to ask questions in class, and she gradually stopped trying to keep up with the other students. Luanne Clawson was more assertive in petitioning for special attention. But she was not able to get the help she needed, and Luanne began to realize that the high school she attended just was not equipped to handle the problems of the slower learners:

> It was just too overcrowded at West Roxbury High—like there
> would be thirty, forty kids in one class. And I know it be real hard
> on the teacher to teach one, you know, and still keep the whole
> class goin'. They have these special-ed classes, I found out about,
> where you can get more help. But when I ask about 'em, you know,
> I found out they was only for kids that was really bad off—can't
> read or nothin'. But some people learn slow, some learn fast, you
> know? And so many kids can't hardly keep up. I don't know *what*
> they could do about it. Way it is now, I think it's real hard on the
> teacher. 'Cause she can't just *stop* everything for one special person,
> you know—she can't hardly slow down all the others.

While young people such as Sandy, Jack, and Douglas wished that their teachers had left them alone and let them structure their own learning programs, the slower learners in our group said they would have liked more individual attention and interaction with their high school teachers. Bobby Jones told me:

> I *like* for a teacher to push me a little—be on my back sometimes, you know? I like for people to come out and talk to me—to tell me, "You're smart, you can do something' with yourself!" I wish I'd've had teachers like that, who come out and told me that I could do it. Then it would of been no problem doin' the work, you know? I *could've* done it—it's just that I *didn't*. I like to get individual attention. I think I could work better if it was just me and the teacher—that way I could stop and ask questions, you know?

Some students I interviewed, who had problems with their teachers and difficulty with their studies, were able to compensate for their poor academic performance by participating in the social life of the school. Excelling in sports is a way for young men, especially, to achieve recognition among their high school classmates. Bobby Jones says the only time he really enjoyed school was when he was a star on the junior high school basketball team. Being eliminated from the freshman football squad for poor grades was a major blow for Bobby.

Todd Clinton says that sports were particularly important in the Portland high school he attended, and he thinks his own lack of interest and involvement in athletics put him at a big social disadvantage:

> That school was really big on sports. The jocks were like the kings of the school—which didn't impress me too much, because they were always trying to impress everybody else. I wasn't a real long-hair or negative person in high school, but I didn't play ball. I would talk to jocks and everything, but I just didn't like their attitudes much—you know, "I can do anything and you're nothing"—I didn't like that attitude. They treated everyone else like a piece of shit. But, you know, I still treated them good—as well as they would have treated me, if I'd have been a jock.

While some of the young people in our group had friends when they were in high school and said they had enjoyed the social aspects of student life, more than half described themselves as loners. Some, such as Douglas Giscard and Sven Latoka, said they thought the high school social scene was pointless and they had removed themselves by choice. Others said they wanted to be accepted but just couldn't seem to make friends or find a way to fit in with the other students.

Peggy Bromfield's parents discouraged involvement with people outside the family when she was a child. By the time she reached the ninth grade, Peggy tended to avoid social situations as much as possible. School was a constant ordeal. She was self-conscious about her appearance and ill-equipped to handle the teasing of her classmates. When things got too uncomfortable for her at school, Peggy would just stay away:

> I was always a loner—no really close friends and just a few acquaintances. I hated to go to school, 'cause I seemed to get hassled a lot by some of the other kids. I got so I never went to English class, 'cause they harassed me. Those boys in there called me Wilma Flintstone, 'cause they said my teeth looked like the stone age. I'd skip classes, and then I'd get called into the office for truancy. I finally told my counselor about what was going on, and she said, "Peggy, have you ever thought that those boys might really like you—that this might be their way of expressing interest in you?" I thought about that, and I decided that she was crazy. I don't think they liked me at all!

Some of the young people I interviewed had faced harassment at school that was far more threatening and pervasive than anything Peggy encountered. During my visits to Boston I met dozens of teen-agers who had been bused from their black neighborhoods and housing projects in Dorchester and Roxbury to schools in South Boston and other white neighborhoods as part of the citywide school desegregation effort. The court-ordered busing plan went into effect in 1975, and young people such as Adam Sledge, who received their transfer papers during the second year of busing, knew they were in for trouble.

Three years later, Adam's memories of this time were still vivid:

> South Boston High when they was integratin'—that was a *rough* time! It was like bein' a nigger in the fifties. It was a real dangerous time. All those people in South Boston say they *hate* niggers, you know? Couldn't hardly walk down the corridor to that school but what you'd get jumped! *They* started all that. Ain't *nobody* wanted to be bused.
>
> From the first I heard about it—when I first got my busin' papers and all—I knew it was gonna be bad. 'Cause they had the idea that *we* did it to 'em, you know? Like *we* made the rules or somethin'. But *we* didn't wanna come to their school as much as *they* didn't want us to be there, you know?

Several of the young people I interviewed had refused to be bused. When Felisa Santana came back to Boston from Puerto Rico and discovered that she had been assigned to South Boston High, she decided not to return to public school. "I knew there would just be riots every day up there," Felisa told me, "The white people there didn't want us Puerto Ricans or blacks in their school, 'cause they're so prejudiced."

Genetta Burke did not want to go to South Boston High either. She received her "busing papers" in the mail two weeks before she was to start the tenth grade, and her mother tried, without success, to get her a transfer. Genetta told me:

> I remember the morning when it finally come down to goin'. Even though I was too old to cry, I stood outside near the buses and cried 'cause my mother made me go to school. I seen all the reports on TV. I knew it was gonna be bad, and I just didn't wanna go there.

Genetta was frightened when she got on the bus, and her experiences in South Boston confirmed her fears. During her nine months as a student at South Boston High, she encountered persistent hostility and frequent acts of violence:

> Everybody called us niggers. They stood out on the sidewalks, yellin' and throwin' stuff at us when we come down the hill by the school. There were grown people out there, wavin' bananas at us, shoutin' stuff like, "Hey monkey, want your food?" They was bombin' the buses and throwin' stuff. Yeah, I was scared—sure I was!
>
> I think the teachers cared—some of 'em anyway. But, you know, the way it was, you couldn't hardly study. Because if there was like a bad group of white people behind you, you know, they would start trouble. In the classrooms, there was like only two or three blacks and all the rest white—so, you know, there was nothin' you could do really. Sometimes they'd just start throwin' chairs and stuff at you—stuff like that—and there was not much you could do about it.
>
> I got trapped up there one day. It was the day that a white guy got stabbed, and the whites trapped everybody up in the school. Yeah, I was right behind him when he got stabbed too. They trapped us in there, and we couldn't get out. They had hockey sticks, rocks, and bats—and we didn't have nothin'. They almost got us, you know? We was in there for hours, but the police finally got us out through a side door.

When Harold Thomas moved into the Victoria Point housing project in December 1976 he was issued busing papers and assigned to South Boston High. He knew little about the school desegregation situation in Boston and was hardly aware of the controversy over busing. Nothing in his past experience prepared him for the hostility he was to encounter at South Boston High. Harold said:

The school I went to in Virginia was integrated, but there was never any real problems there. Yeah, well, I seen maybe one or two situations—problems that you might call racial. Some people were prejudiced there, and each group—black and white—tended to stick to its own some. But at school, it didn't really matter to no one whether you was black or white.

When I got up here, I found out that white people could hate you just because you was black. It just didn't make any sense at all for people to feel like that! When they first started comin' down on me at school, I tried to walk away. But I couldn't help it, I *had* to end up fightin'. When somebody jumps on me, I can't just sit there and let 'em beat me up, you know? So I fought back. Sometimes seemed like all I did at that school was fight.

Adam Sledge attended South Boston High during the same year as Harold, and he also felt that fighting back was the only way he could respond to the situation:

When they said nigger this and nigger that, I just walk on by 'em—until they put their hands on me! Then I had no choice but to fight, 'cause I wasn't gettin' myself hurt. I had to watch my brother and my sister too, you know? They was goin' there too. And if they know you got family there, they try to get to you by gettin' your family. It got to where I was fightin' most every day up there.

Integration is supposed to improve the quality of education for non-white students, and, undoubtedly there are cases where it has. But the desegregation of Boston's schools seems to have negatively affected many of the students involved. It disrupted rather than enhanced their education. The young people who had to leave their neighborhoods and fight their way through school in alien territory could not see much point in busing.

Few of the black teen-agers I met who had been assigned to South Boston High stayed there for more than one year. Harold Thomas got tired of fighting—he dropped out of school and joined the army reserves. Genetta Burke became pregnant toward the end of her first year at South Boston. She was able to transfer into a special maternity school, where she completed the eleventh grade. After the baby was born, she dropped out of school rather than return to South Boston High. Adam Sledge was able to get a transfer to a technical high school, where he spent two months in the eleventh grade before dropping out. Adam's sister stopped going to school midway through the year. She stayed at home until she was able to get a transfer for the next school year. Adam's brother left school for good during his first year at South Boston High.

What Is School For?

> All my life, I was told that school was important. Grades were
> a big thing with my parents—they like to brag about my brother
> and all. If we got good grades, we got money—like for each "A" we
> got a dollar, and a "B" was fifty cents. When my grades started
> slidin', I didn't get any money. But by that time I didn't really care. I
> couldn't see the point of it. I mean, what was it all for anyway?
> *Sven Latoka*

Not all of the young people I interviewed had parents who were as
concerned about grades as Sven's. But most of them had been told in a
variety of ways that their performance in school was an important issue—and grades were the measure of how well they performed. Sven was
not the only one who could not see the point. Some of those in our group
knew they would never get good grades no matter how hard they worked.
Others claimed they could easily have excelled if grades had really mat-
tered to them. But by the time they reached the final months of their
incomplete high school careers, most of them, like Sven, had given up
trying.

They complained about the emphasis placed on grades, as opposed
to learning, in high school. But behind these complaints lay questions
about the purpose of much of what they were required to study. They had
been told by their teachers and parents that the things they learned in
school would prepare them for later life. Most of these high school dropouts
acknowledged the value of obtaining basic reading, writing, and math
skills. But they could not see how many of the things they did in school
could be of any use to them later on. Most of the slow learners I talked with
seemed to have particularly disliked the required English classes. They
believed that most of what they studied in these classes was pointless, as
Carrie Green put it:

> Fundamentals of English—who cares! I don't think that's something
> you should really have to take. Like diagramming sentences. I
> mean, how often do you need to do something like that in life? But
> it seemed like, in school, they wanted you to do things like that
> over and over.

Sven Latoka could not see how English composition could be of
much use to a construction worker:

> I agree that a person needs to read and write. Everybody needs
> *some* English—just to talk and all. But I don't like to write, just to
> be writing. I'm a carpenter, and I don't need to be writing com-

positions, you know? All that stuff about nouns, pronouns, verbs, adverbs. It just seems really confusing and unnecessary to me.

Even those with stronger academic interests than Sven and Carrie were apt to doubt the value of many of the things they were supposed to learn in high school. History was frequently viewed as irrelevant. "It just didn't make any sense," Jack Thrush told me, "I don't understand why you would need to know about things way back in the past." Many of these teen-agers seemed to lack patience for any material that they could not relate directly to their immediate interests or circumstances, and some viewed the materials chosen for the high school curriculum with particular skepticism. Douglas Giscard said:

> A lot of things we were supposed to learn in school just didn't
> seem necessary, and some of it was just ridiculous. Some of the in-
> formation you'd read in the textbooks seemed old—out-of-date or
> something. Everything always had a moral, you know? It was like
> it wasn't *real.* I don't know quite how to explain it, but I'd find my-
> self reading things and kinda wondering, "Maybe this is right, or
> maybe it isn't."

Most of the young people in our group felt that high school ill-prepared them for life. Those who had been out of school for any length of time had typically discovered there were many things they needed to know that had not been taught in school. Sandy Bonds observed that:

> They oughta teach you how to handle yourself as an adult—fi-
> nancially and other ways—instead of leading you around by the
> nose. They should teach you how to make a decision on your own,
> how to rent an apartment, how to talk to people when you're bein'
> interviewed for a job, how to read and understand contracts—
> things like that. You know? Like what to do with your bank
> account, and where to get the best deals. Even down to shop-
> ping—I mean, they oughta teach a person how to shop for gro-
> ceries. A lot of people don't know how.

Many high schools offer courses in vocational education, career exploration, personal finance, consumer economics, and other subjects geared to practical, rather than academic, applications. But most of the young people in our group said they did not have access to courses of this sort. Some of them, undoubtedly, left school without ever realizing that such courses were available. Some of them had attended inner-city schools, where the dwindling tax base and declining enrollment had resulted in budgets that pared the secondary curriculum to the bone. Others, who had problems with their academic performance or their behavior in school, claimed they were passed over for participation in special courses and were shunted into general programs. Jack Thrush told me:

> I thought school was supposed to prepare you for life. But from what I've seen, you gotta be one of the so-called better students just to get into these classes where they teach you business, job skills, and all that stuff. I wanted to learn things that would help me when I went out to get a job, but I was one of the people who was screwin' off a lot—just lettin' it slide. And if you're not a good student, they just put you into these plain classes that are real boring.

Jack seems to have validly appraised the situation in many schools. In years past, slower students and underachievers—particularly those from low-income families—were often channeled out of the general high school program and into occupational training schools or vocational programs, while the better students were encouraged to prepare themselves for college by taking academic courses. But many students have come to believe that vocational training and practical skills afford greater advantages in today's job market than academic achievement. Students are clamoring for vocational preparation, career planning, and work experience. But, given the budget restrictions limiting these services in many high schools, those identified as troublemakers or less-able students are often excluded.

While several of the young people in our group had taken one or two vocational courses in school, such as typing or shop classes, Todd Clinton was the only one who had received training in a well-equipped facility that introduced him to a number of different occupational skills. At a school district skills center Todd was able to experiment, to develop design-related skills, and to consider a variety of occupational options. Todd considered this experience to be the high point of his high school career:

> I was real lucky to get in this special program. For about a year and a half, I was able to leave my regular school and go to the skills center. The skills center is for kids from three different high schools. It's an OJT type thing. You go out there and you work with real stuff. You get the chance to do things that you *want* to do— things you've always thought about doin'. They've got a mechanics shop, drafting, photography—there's tons of different things out there to do!
>
> For awhile I thought about bein' a draftsman. I was really good at drafting; it was one of my favorite classes. I would go in there, and they would say, "We're gonna draw *this* today." And we would all go to work on it. Sometimes they would say, "Why don't you guys just work up somethin' of your own?" And I would just look at somethin' in the room, and I got so I could just draft it up. I'd do all kinds of things. I drew up desks, walls, chalkboards, houses. . . .

Then I got into photography, and I was thinkin' about becoming a photographer. I did everything from taking pictures to running 'em off. I'd do the whole process. I would take a picture, make the negative, and then I would make a big sheet type thing and run it off on the press.

You know, my counselor didn't want me to get in the program at first. But I think I ended up bein' one of the best students out there! For awhile, I was even a teacher's aide. The head instructor liked me. We really got along. She would let me work on whatever I wanted, you know? And I would turn out some of the neatest work that place had ever seen. They used a lot of my things too. There were pictures I did for the school paper. So, like I say, the head instructor, she was a big influence on me.

They got us to think about what we might do when we left school. They had us go out and look for jobs as a way of finding out about different careers. The time I spent out there was really good for me—much better than the rest of high school. Bein' there was what got me started thinkin' about some kind of career in design, you know?

Dropping Out

Why did I drop out? Well, it's kinda hard to explain. But what it boiled down to was just lack of interest. I didn't just drop right out, you know? Some days I'd be there—some days I wouldn't. Then finally, I just didn't go at all.   *Sven Latoka*

Some dropouts make a sharp break or a dramatic exit from school, but many, like Sven, just gradually stop going. Truancy is a serious problem in today's high schools, particularly in the inner city, where some school officials report average classroom absentee rates as high as 40 percent. Educators recognize that truancy or chronic absenteeism often is a prelude to dropping out. Some students, such as Sven, do not bother to report to school when they do not feel like going. Others come in only to meet their friends and make plans to skip part or all of their classes.

For a student such as Carrie Green, who found school difficult, the temptation to cut class was almost irresistible:

My girlfriend, Michelle—I've known her for years—she skipped school all the time. She'd usually leave third period—just when I was having biology. So every time she'd see me, we'd go off together to the parking lot and ditch class. If it was a nice day, I'd go along with her when she skipped for the rest of the day. It wasn't too smart on my part, 'cause I was havin' a hard enough time already. And with all the skipping I wasn't gettin' any of the work done, and I was flat-out failing. It was bad news! And it finally got to be so much pressure that I just said forget it!

While boredom and academic pressure may make dropping out seem attractive, personal circumstances and family problems also influence the decision to leave school before graduation. Many young women who become pregnant decide to leave school months before the baby is due. Carmeletta DeVries said:

> When I first found out I was pregnant, I was still goin' to school most days, but I wasn't doin' too good. I was bored and I wasn't feelin' good—I just got to the point where I was lazy, and I didn't wanna do nothin'. I was gettin' into trouble, and callin' my mother to come get me. My mother told me she was tired of comin' up to the school. And if I wanted to quit, then quit. 'Cause she was disgusted with me, you know? So I quit.

Prospective parenthood can also make high school seem less important to a young man. When his girlfriend, Cindy, got pregnant, Adam Sledge started staying home from school. He told me:

> Finally I took it upon myself and told my mother, "I'm not goin' back." And she said, "You better go on back there and take care of yourself!" But I told her I was tired of wakin' up every morning, just to go to the school, you know, and just *sit* there. There I was just sittin' in school like a child, and my girl, you know, was havin' a baby. I felt I should be out workin' instead. So I just stopped goin' and that was that!

Todd Clinton was less than three months from graduating when he dropped out of school and joined the National Guard. His decision was triggered by family problems:

> I left school because I *had* to get away. Basically, I had just *had* it with my father. We were fighting all the time, and I couldn't live there anymore. It was either me or him. I *had* to go. I didn't discuss it with anyone at the school. I figgered they'd try to talk me out of it, you know? I had wanted to graduate and all—no one in my family had graduated from high school. But I couldn't see any other way to go.

Harold Thomas dropped out of school in the eleventh grade because he wanted to get out of South Boston High. He requested a transfer, but it did not come through. He thought about going back to Virginia on his own, but felt that he could not abandon his sisters and brother. When he finally decided to join the army reserves, he did not discuss his plans with anyone at the school:

> I didn't go into the office or nothin'. See, I didn't wanna talk to *nobody* up there about it, 'cause I didn't wanna *adjust* to it at school. Way things are up here—I just don't wanna be like that. Way that people up at the school talked—they been livin' up here all their lives—I felt they would try to change my mind or change the way I wanted to live. I decided I'd be better off joinin' the army reserves. So that's what I done.

Those who did discuss their intentions with school counselors, family members, or older friends were warned about the dismal prospects that awaited high school dropouts, but they were usually in no mood to listen. "Yeah, I heard all the bad stuff about dropping out," Jack Thrush told me, "but I didn't really care about it. I just wanted to get out of there." Carmeletta DeVries said, "Nothin' that anyone told me at the time really *got* to me, you know?"

Some of the young people in our group were so disaffected with their parents that they did not care what they thought. A number of them did not tell their parents or other family members what was going on until after they had dropped out, and the announcement sometimes came as a shock. "My dropping out got a *big* reaction at home," Carrie Green said. "They all told me I shouldn't have done it. But it was too late, and I didn't really care what they thought about it."

Douglas Giscard was living on his own when he left school. It was several months before he told his parents he had dropped out, and Douglas said they had a hard time accepting it:

> They always expected me to finish college—that was the big thing with them. They thought I was bright and all. But when they found out I had dropped out of high school, they begged me just to go back and stay till graduation.

What did the young people in our group plan to do when they left school? Harold and Todd went directly into the military. Peggy Bromfield got married. Carmeletta and Genetta had babies on the way. Luanne Clawson enrolled immediately in the CETA youth program at the community center near her home. She said:

> Way I looked on it, I wasn't really droppin' out, you know? I left school 'cause I wasn't really learnin' nothin'. In my classes, the teacher would just pass me over. If I be absent, she would say, "I can't go back to that work right now—I give it to you later." But when later comes, she never give it to me. So I just say to my-

self, you know, "Hey, I'll just go on over to the CETA program."
I heard about it all the time on the radio, and I knew some kids
there that liked it. So I thought maybe, you know, I could get
more out of it than what I was gettin' at school.

Some of the young people had no immediate plans, they just wanted
to get out of school. "I was at a radical stage," Douglas told me. "I didn't
really know what I wanted or what I was going to do." Most of them
intended to find work and get by on their own. Though they did not expect
it to be easy, they were often startled to discover how bleak the job outlook
was for a teen-ager with only nine or ten years of schooling and no employment experience. Sandy Bonds said:

> I knew some people got by without finishing high school, and I
> thought I'd try it. I was tired of goin' to school. I wanted to do other
> things like writin' songs, travelin', and tryin' to get a job. Found out
> that was impossible, really. Our social makeup actually forces you
> to go to school. Nobody wants to hire you for anything worthwhile
> unless you have that diploma. I guess they figure just because you
> have ideas and you've read a couple books—that doesn't tell me
> you're smart enough to work.

By the time they enrolled in employment and training programs,
most of the young people in our group had been out of school for several
years. They had had some rough times and often were willing to testify to
the error of their ways: "They was all right about it. I guess I should've
listened"; "I was a dummy to quit"; "Dropping out is a big mistake." Such
comments seem to be almost obligatory for struggling dropouts who turn
to employment and training programs for help. Did they really regret their
decisions to leave school? Yes and no.
    Yes, their experiences after leaving school had convinced them that
employers do care about secondary credentials, and most of them wished
they had graduated. But would they be willing to return to high school and
face again the problems they had encountered there? In most cases, the
answer was no. Though they had grown to hate the stigma of being a
dropout and believed that their lack of a diploma barred them from having
been considered for better jobs, most of them felt that leaving high school
was a decision they had to make. As Adam Sledge said:

> If I could turn back the clock, you know, it probably wouldn't be
> any different. Even at the time I didn't really feel it was a *good*
> choice, you know? But it was somethin' I felt I *had* to do. There just
> wasn't nothin' happenin' with me and school anymore.

Getting a Secondary Credential

High school graduation does not guarantee a good job, but youth employment and training programs generally operate on the assumption that a secondary credential is a prerequisite for employability. The CETA programs that I studied offered part-time subsidized jobs as an incentive for students to stay in high school until graduation. However, the programs were not generally successful in luring dropouts back into regular high school programs. Some CETA programs for dropouts coupled part-time work experience with daily academic instruction provided in the community center or program facility. Other programs released participants from full-time CETA jobs for several hours each week to participate in General Equivalency Diploma (GED) classes. Some of the young people in our group enrolled in full-time work or training programs with no provisions or requirements for academic instruction, but they were generally encouraged to attend GED classes provided in the evening at nearby community colleges, schools, or neighborhood agencies.

By the time they enrolled in employment and training programs most of the young people in our group were willing to at least try to study for a GED. Felisa Santana and Luanne Clawson saw CETA-subsidized GED programs as an alternative to high school enrollment. Bobby Jones and Carmeletta DeVries viewed GED instruction as a first step in preparing for the world of work. Sven Latoka and Adam Sledge felt that a GED certificate might give them a competitive edge in their job search. Harold Thomas wanted to be accepted into the regular army and had been told by his recruiter that he needed a GED in order to qualify for special training assignments. Jean Ansel and Douglas Giscard wanted to go to college one day and knew they would need a secondary credential. Jack Thrush and Genetta Burke said they enrolled voluntarily in GED classes because they wanted to prove to themselves and their families that they could finish school. All of these young people had problems in high school. How well did they do in the GED programs?

A substantial portion, including some who left school as early as ninth grade and had been away for as long as two and a half years, were able to pass their GED examinations with minimal preparation and surprising ease. Several were able to prepare themselves successfully in a matter of weeks. Douglas Giscard said:

> I was really surprised at how light the classes were. I was supposed to take the eight-week preparation course. I studied for about two weeks, and they said it was all right; I was ready to take the test. When I finally got to take it about a month later, I passed all the exams within about three hours!

While few dropouts pass the GED examinations as easily as Douglas did, about half of the young people in our group obtained their GED certificates after less than six months of study. Most of these young people found the process to be less painful than they had expected. Though they usually were required to attend scheduled classes, they did not have to fit into a traditional classroom environment. They were given packaged learning materials, were able to consult with an instructor on an individual basis, and were allowed to proceed at their own pace.

Jack Thrush took his GED instruction at the youth program agency in Kalamazoo. Studying two hours a day, four days a week was not easy for Jack, but he stuck with it for eight weeks. Math gave him the most trouble; he was able to move through the other subjects with relative ease. He worried about the examinations—friends had told him they were difficult—and he was delighted when he passed them on the first try, with above average scores in each subject.

Sven Latoka had never liked studying. But he decided to get a GED, and he was willing to work for it. He attended evening classes at a local high school, twice a week for four months. Sven said:

> I took a sixteen-week course. Can't say I *liked* it, you know? But it was better than what I expected. For one thing the lady who taught it—the instructor—was pretty good. She helped you out when you was having trouble, but they didn't treat you, you know, like a *kid* or anything like that. Seemed like it was easier than school—but then I *did* study for it at home, and I did not do that in high school, you know? I wanted to get it over with as fast as I could. Took a while longer than I wanted, but I got it.

Several of the young people in our group went into longer-term, more intensive GED programs. Felisa Santana took courses in English, math, Hispanic culture and history, and office skills at a bilingual community-based high school. She went to school there for three semesters—attending classes two to four hours a day—before taking her GED examinations. Luanne Clawson and Bobby Jones were both enrolled in a community center-based CETA project, which coupled four hours of daily academic instruction with part-time work experience. While some of the young people in this program were preparing to take the GED examinations, others, like Bobby, had substantial academic deficiencies and needed intensive remedial help.

Bobby had dropped out of the ninth grade. When he enrolled in the CETA project at the community center, he had been out of school for more than two years, and he lacked the skills and discipline to tackle high school-level studies. His instructor, Mr. Morelock, told me: "Bobby reads at the level of a third- or fourth-grade student, and he's just as far behind in math. He's smart enough—he can learn—but it's been a long time since he applied himself to anything." After nine months of remedial instruction, Bobby was still far from ready for his GED examinations. But his reading and writing skills had improved, and Bobby was excited about the progress he had made in the program:

> I'm workin' hard, and I think I've done real good in here. It been so long since I was in school that I don't really remember if high school was harder or easier than this. But I'll tell you one thing— in here, we do more work than I ever did in a *long* time. It's good for me here, you know? I get all the help I need from missin' all that school. When I was in school before, you know, I wouldn't ask the teacher for nothin'—if I didn't know it, I just didn't do it—that was a big mistake. Here, there isn't many people in the class —so the teacher can help me out. We got one teacher in here, right? He get *around* to all of us, too, you know? Like he talks to us, and he goes over the work with us. He says, "Anyone have any problems, you know you can come to me for help, individually."

There was some disagreement among those who completed a GED about whether the certificate they received was really the equivalent of a high school diploma. Some of the GED completers felt that employers would not think their certificates were as good as a diploma. Most of these young people believed that the GED represented about the same level of skill that an average student would have attained upon completion of a general program in most high schools. But as Douglas Giscard said, "It sure didn't cover all the college prep material." Several of the young people wanted to go on to college or other postsecondary programs and wondered if their GED instruction would be adequate preparation. Felisa Santana felt she lacked the background in history and science that most college-bound students would have had. But Jean Ansel had no problems enrolling in Portland Community College and did well in the evening classes she took there. While Douglas agreed that the GED would "get you into any junior college or community college," he was afraid that private colleges and universities would not consider it an acceptable credential.

Three of the young people in our group, Carmeletta DeVries, Carrie Green, and Sandy Bonds, did not get their GEDs during the time they were enrolled in CETA programs. In addition to her job assignment at a Kalamazoo hospital, Carmeletta signed up for GED instruction at the youth program agency, but she dropped out after several weeks of class. She said, "Workin' all day and goin' to school nights didn't leave me no time to be with the baby or get anything done at home." Carrie left the CETA program without ever taking the GED classes. "I wanna get a GED someday," Carrie told me, "I need it. But I know it's gonna be real hard for me to get, and I'm just not ready to do it right now." Sandy said her CETA counselor talked her into starting a GED preparation program, but she stopped going before she was ready to take her examinations:

> I was barely used to workin' all day, and I sure wasn't ready to be sittin' in class all night. I was falling asleep in there! I'm getting skills on the job, and I'll learn the other stuff I need to know. But I don't see where I need some little piece of paper that says I did it.

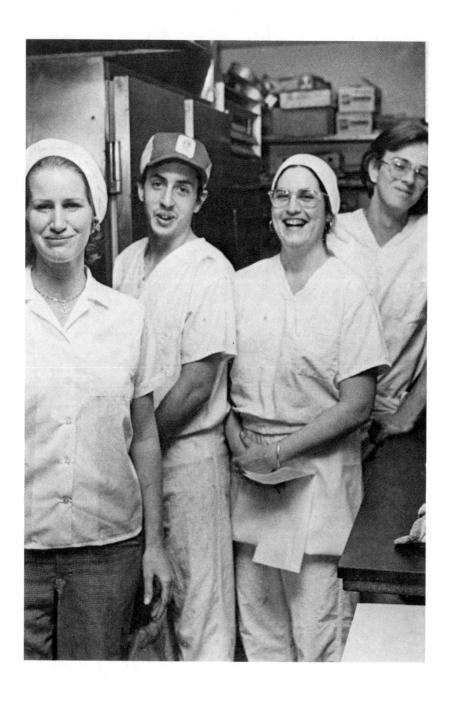

5. Looking at the World of Work

The School of Hard Knocks

> People say that all it takes to succeed is hard work. You know how you hear all these stories about people who start out with nothin' and work their way up the ladder? Well, let me tell you something: Maybe it was like that once upon a time, but it doesn't seem to work that way anymore. If you're young and you don't have much experience, nobody wants to really give you a chance—they don't even wanna *look* at you. I been out there and I know.   *Carrie Green*

Like many of the other young people I interviewed, Carrie does not need to be told how difficult the working world can be for a teen-ager who lacks experience, credentials, and connections. Nearly half of the other young people in our group were out working or looking for work long before they signed up for youth employment programs. These teen-agers had the chance to get a close-up view of the world of work—they were thrown into it with little preparation. Their experiences did not foster optimism or self-confidence.

Carrie was sixteen when she started her working life in a plastics factory, but she did not stay for long. For nearly two years she moved from job to job, without finding one that she liked or was able to keep. Carrie talks about her experience in a matter-of-fact way:

> Compared to most kids my age, I think I know more about the world and about workin'. It's really rough out there, and I found that out young. When I got my first job at the Blasco plant, I was barely sixteen, but I lied and told 'em I was eighteen. I was makin' $2.90 an hour there, and I thought the money was real good at the time. But, you know, it wasn't really worth it.
>
> It was summertime when I worked at Blasco, and they had these big machines we worked on for molding hot plastic. It was a lot of hard work; it would get to be like a hundred and thirty degrees in there! August was really the worst. We was all havin' a hard time by then. After I'd been there about three months, I got real sick and had to stay home for a week. Just when I was about ready to come back to work, they called and told me I was laid off. I talked to my

boss about it, and he said I should come back later in the fall and they would probably put me back on. So I come back. But I screwed up—they give me these papers to fill out and stuff, and I forgot and wrote my real birthdate. When they asked me about it, I tried to tell 'em I had made a mistake. But by that time they had it figured out that I was lyin'.

After that, the jobs I got were mostly in restaurants. I'd work like in the kitchen. At this one place, I was a salad girl—I'd cut up all the stuff, and keep the salad bar filled up. I liked that job pretty good, but I got into a fight with my boss and I quit. Another place, I got fired for usin' the telephone. See, I couldn't drive yet, so when I worked nights, I had to call up somebody and get a ride home. Every night I'd ask permission, and they would let me go in and use this phone in the office. One night my boss wasn't around or anything, so I just went in to use the phone. He come in while I was on the phone and started yellin' at me, said I wasn't supposed to be in there without permission and that I shouldn't be talkin' on the phone during work time. We was almost through workin' and I tried to explain, but he got real mad and told me to go home and not bother comin' back.

I had a real hard time findin' work after that. I was willing to do almost anything, but I just couldn't seem to find a job.

Jack Thrush also got his first full-time job at age sixteen. Like Carrie, he was eager to work and be out on his own, and he was willing to start out on the bottom:

First job I got was bein' a busboy, and I was pretty happy about it. It was at one of the bigger restaurants in Kalamazoo. You were supposed to be eighteen to work there, and apparently they just hired me 'cause they needed somebody right then. As soon as they got an application with somebody eighteen, they laid me off. I kept lookin' for jobs on my own. I had a couple of part-time, temporary deals, you know? And finally I got this dishwasher job—it was steady and paid $2.00 an hour. I thought that was great! I worked there about five months. But then—I don't know—I started to want a better job. I was makin' below minimum wage, and I was only workin' part-time. I don't think he was really payin' us fair for all the work we had to do. It really wasn't good at all. So I looked around, tryin' to find a better job—or the same kind of job at a better place. But I didn't have much luck.

By the time they came to the youth program agency in Kalamazoo, both Carrie and Jack had been unemployed for several months. They wanted full-time work at minimum wage, but they had no vocational preferences. Like many of the young people I interviewed, they were thinking in terms of a job, rather than a career. Jack told me:

> I just wanted a job, you know? They told me this was a program to get you work experience, you know, give you an income, some kind of training, and maybe finish school and all. I just listened to all that. They said a bunch of things, and I listened to 'em, but I didn't really think much about it. My main objective was just to get a job.

Sven Latoka knew what he wanted to do before he came to the CETA program. He had training and work experience as a carpenter's helper, and he wanted to be a carpenter like his father had been. But Sven was only seventeen when his father left the construction business to work on a fishing boat, and he could not find work on his own as a carpenter, so he took whatever work he could get. He was looking for a steady job, and he was not too excited about participating in a program. Sven told me:

> I wouldn't have come here if I'd have known I could get a better job somewhere else—no way. 'Cause they told me this was a *learning* program, you know? I wasn't real sure what that meant, but I already *knew* how to work. I knew somethin' about the workin' world. I'd been out there, gettin' jobs and tryin' to get jobs for a long time.
>   The best time I had workin' was with my dad. I learned a lot from him about carpentry, and I think I'm pretty good at it. But if you're sixteen or seventeen years old, nobody seems to want to hire you as a carpenter. And when you give your father as a reference, nobody seems to take it serious, you know?
>   But still I needed to work, you know? So I did just about any-thing—physical work, washin' dishes, pick up trash—anything, really. I bounced around from job to job, but I don't think I was ever out of a job more than a week. Most jobs I just plain got sick of—fed up with. Too little pay, too much work for the money—I couldn't find any job that was really interesting. I worked hard, you know, *that* was never the problem. One time I went down to a labor pool—on Albany Street I think it was. They had me out unloading hundred-pound sacks of flour off a train for about twelve hours straight! I got minimum wage for that one. I don't think I've ever had as hard a day's work in my life!

Jean Ansel and Douglas Giscard also spent time in the labor force before coming to the CETA program. Both had been able to find jobs on their own, but they had grown dissatisfied with the kind of work they were doing. During her struggle to free herself from alcohol, drug dependency, and life on the street, Jean worked—first as a waitress and later as a clerk in a discount store. She felt that she had learned from this experience and was ready to try something else. After his burglary conviction, Douglas worked as a dishwasher and a delivery boy. Though he had no specific plans, Douglas was looking for work that offered more challenge and wider possibilities for the future:

> I was bored with the kind of work I'd been doing, and I wanted to find something better to do with my time. I started thinking about the future, you know? I saw people out there who were thirty, thirty-five years old, working in those kinds of jobs, going nowhere! And I knew I didn't want that to happen to me.

Tien Van Chin had also begun to worry about the future. Like Douglas and Jean, he was dissatisfied with the kind of work he had been able to get, but did not think another job was the answer. Tien had come to the United States determined to succeed. But, in addition to his youth and lack of credentials, he faced language and cultural barriers. Though he began working almost as soon as he arrived in Portland, Tien was not able to find a job that offered the opportunity for advancement. After nearly two years in the secondary labor market, Tien had decided that hard work was not enough:

> When I was growing up in my country, I go to school but I don't have to work. Here, I'm working all the time! I work hard. At first I don't mind. I study English at night and think it will get better. I do work like dishwasher, car washer, busboy—thing like that. I never keep those jobs long because I don't want to be doing that type job. So I quit to get another. I want *better* job, but I would end up with just *different* job. Soon I realize that if I don't continue with my education—get some training—I will be unable to get better job. I will be always busboy and stuff like that—always get the menial job. So I don't forget that, and I decide some way to go to school—get a better skill.

While some of the young people in our group had been out working or looking for work for several years before they heard about youth employment and training programs, others were still outside the labor force, looking for a way to get in. Some of them wanted to get started right away. Sandy Bonds, Adam Sledge, and Carmeletta DeVries needed immediate income and came to CETA agencies seeking full-time jobs. Others thought it would take time to get ready: Felisa Santana, Luanne Clawson, and Bobby Jones all thought a secondary credential was important and were willing to defer full-time employment while they went back to school.

But none of these people knew much about what they wanted, or even what was possible for them, in the world of work. "I didn't know what I wanted to work *as*," admitted Sandy Bonds, "I learned how to get by on the street, but *working*—I just plain don't know much about it."

Though they had no experience in the regular labor force, some of these teen-agers had been in CETA summer programs, which provided part-time work experience during school vacations. The summer before he left school, Bobby worked as a kitchen aide in the community center lunch program. Felisa Santana had been a recreation aide at a summertime daycamp, operated by a community-based agency in Boston. Luanne Clawson, who had worked as a first-aid assistant at a similar camp, said her job had consisted of "washin' cuts and puttin' bandages on kids who got hurt." While these young people enjoyed their summers in the CETA program, they typically failed to see any connection between their experiences there and what they might face in a "real" job. Carmeletta DeVries said:

> I got in the CETA summer program when I was fifteen. I got my choice of what to do, and I picked clerical. They put me over at the county building—but it wasn't really like a job or anything, you know? They put me down in the basement on the copy machine. Nobody really talked to me much. I would just be down there in the basement, copying all mornin', or sometimes they let me sort mail—just real easy stuff. It was okay, you know? I was real glad to get the money. But I didn't learn that much about what it would be like to have a *real* job.

Carmeletta's ten weeks as a clerical aide was the only work experience she had before enrolling full-time in the Kalamazoo CETA program. But the two other single mothers in our group, Genetta Burke and Peggy Bromfield, had both worked in unsubsidized jobs. Genetta's jobs as a receptionist and an assembly worker had been short-term—she did not want to risk losing her AFDC benefits. Peggy's time in the labor force also had been short. When she got her first job in a garment factory, she was sixteen years old, had a five-month-old son, and was pregnant with her second child. Her marriage was breaking up, and Peggy was trying to get off welfare:

> I needed full-time work, but it was hard to think of anything I could actually do. I applied for jobs as a salesgirl and a waitress, but I got turned down for 'em 'cause I didn't have any experience. But I've always been pretty good at sewing, you know? So I went in to this factory, and I really caught on quick there. I was probably the best

sewer in the factory. After only a few weeks, I was puttin' out more ponchos than anybody else in the place. They even gave me a merit raise. But then they said you had to work overtime, and you couldn't keep your job if you didn't. I tried to do it. But it meant I was away from Jared, my baby, for twelve hours every day, and I just couldn't do that, so I quit.

After that I went to work for another sewing factory down the street. I walked two miles a day to get there and back. I told the guy there, "I'm experienced. You pay me $2.75 to start, and I want a raise in a month." He paid me the $2.75, but when a month came, he just gave me a line—sayin' I did this and that wrong and wasn't doin' any good. I ask him what he meant by that, and he said he always saw me rippin' out all these seams. But, you know, everybody on my line was always passin' their errors to me 'cause I could rip 'em out real fast. I'd been doin' all these errors for everyone else. He knew that, too. But he wouldn't give me a raise, so I decided to quit that job. It just wasn't worth it.

Both Genetta and Peggy were interested in full-time employment, but neither felt she was qualified for the kind of job that would be worth the benefits she would lose and the difficulties she would face in going to work. These young women wanted a chance to find out more about different job opportunities and requirements, and to improve and broaden their skills before going back into the job market.

Getting a Program Assignment

The young people in our group came to youth employment and training programs with varying levels of exposure to the world of work and with a range of needs and expectations. While some of them had managed to keep their heads above water in the unskilled labor pool, others had yet to get their feet wet. Some of these teen-agers had urgent needs for income and were willing to consider any job that would help keep them going. Others were looking for something more: they wanted job experience, vocational skills, or educational credentials that would help them to build a better future. Few of them had specific plans or occupational goals. When they came to youth program agencies for help, most had only vague ideas about what kinds of opportunities were available and what they could expect to gain from program participation.

What did the programs have to offer these young people? Federally funded youth employment and training programs are intended to both meet immediate job and income needs and improve the longer-term employment prospects of the young people they serve. In the hope that local program sponsors will develop comprehensive systems that can meet a range of needs, federal legislation has authorized a variety of activities, including academic instruction, vocational training, career information and counseling, job search and survival training, and placement and follow-up services, as well as subsidized work experience. Most program agencies offer young people some choice in job assignments and activities, but relatively few have the resources to provide a spectrum of services or the capability to tailor job assignments and package supportive services on an individual basis. The young people in our group who were most satisfied with their program assignments were those who knew what they wanted before they enrolled and had the good fortune to apply through a program agency that was equipped to provide the services they needed.

Sven Latoka wanted a full-time construction job. He applied directly to a CETA building-renovation project operated by a neighborhood agency in Jamaica Plain. Though he would have preferred a regular job in the construction industry, he had not been able to find one; and Sven felt his work experience assignment was an acceptable alternative:

> It was a way to get back to the kind of work I like best—get back to bein' a carpenter. I wasn't too impressed with the money. I knew they was only payin' minimum wage, you know? But they said it would last for ten months, and that sounded real good to me. I was tired of bouncing from job to job, and I figured with the experience I would get—if I proved myself here— I'd have that much better chance when I got through with the program.

Todd Clinton also knew what he wanted. He had decided to become a hair stylist. But he needed help and he did not know where to get it. He had quit his job with his father's construction company to enroll in the Belle Vista Hair Design Academy. After paying his first-term tuition and buying the uniform-style clothes he needed for school, Todd had no money to support himself and no way to pay for subsequent tuition. He'd been living with friends since the break with his father, and one of his roommates suggested that he check out the possibilities for tuition support from an employment and training program.

When he walked into Portland's Southeast youth service center, Todd knew little about the CETA program:

> I came to the center because I heard something about this Basic Grant Program and I thought maybe they could help me get some kind of grant for school. But while I was there, I found out from this booklet they gave me that I was eligible for this CETA youth program. I had heard about CETA and I thought they just gave

people jobs, but this book said they also had vocational training. I didn't know whether they would pay for cosmetology school, but I decided it was worth a shot.

The center offered a variety of services to eligible young people, including tuition payments and stipends for those enrolled in approved vocational training programs in public or private schools. Todd's cosmetology program met the approval criteria. In fact, the center's CETA program was already providing support for several students at the Belle Vista Hair Design Academy. Despite his family's income, Todd qualified for the CETA program. He was nineteen, unemployed, and living on his own. But Todd said the staff at the center had to be convinced that his intentions were serious before they would accept his application:

> I didn't just walk in off the street and they gave me a bunch of money—it wasn't like that at all. First I went in several times to talk to one of the counselors, Robbie Anderson. Robbie talked to me about the program—what it was for and what they were able to do—and he asked me a bunch of questions about school and what my plans for the future were. Finally, about the third time I came back, he told me that I would have to talk to the program director, Jack Bugati. And he kinda warned me that I should get ready for it, 'cause I would have to prove myself to Bugati—convince him that I was really serious about school.
>
> *That* interview was really tough! Bugati pretty much put it right to me. What he said to me, basically, was: "You want our money? Tell me why we should give you anything." I told him I didn't want anything handed to me. I was goin' to school, and I was willing to work hard. He asked me why I wanted to be a hair stylist, and I told him some of my ideas about hair design and what I wanted to do. It was kinda weird, really. In some ways, I felt like he was givin' me the runaround, but I could tell he was really listenin' to what I said. Anyway, like I said, he seemed real negative. But then all of a sudden—after I got done talking to him—he just kinda stood up, and that was it! Just like that, he said, "We'll draw up the papers, and you can start collecting your stipend in two weeks." I really felt good, because I knew where I was headed and I knew I was gonna make it. I had really wanted to do it, and somebody had made it possible.

Some of the other young people in our group, who were less certain than Sven or Todd about what they wanted, simply settled for whatever program services were most readily available. This was particularly true for the teen-agers from Boston who enrolled directly in CETA projects.

Adam Sledge and Harold Thomas were both looking for work when they saw the sign in the Victoria Point community center announcing jobs on a CETA weatherization project. Adam was eager to get started on some kind of full-time job. Harold wanted temporary employment while he studied for a GED. Neither had any particular interest in learning weatherization or construction skills. They enrolled in the CETA project because it provided full-time work at minimum wage, had no education or skill requirements, and was based in their own housing project.

Genetta was no longer living in Victoria Point when she heard about the weatherization project from an acquaintance who was one of the work crew supervisors. She was not looking for work at the time, and her recruitment into the project seems to have been almost accidental:

> I didn't really know Henry *well*, but I had met him last summer, right? Well, one Sunday, I went over to the store to get a newspaper, and I saw him there. He asked me did I want to get in this new project they was openin' up at Victoria Point. They was tryin' to hire eighteen people, and they didn't have enough yet. He asked me did I want to come over to the community center the next day and sign up for it. So I just came. I was tired of sittin' home every day doin' nothin', and I thought earnin' some extra money would do me some good. I thought maybe it would be somethin' that could help me work into a regular job. I was a little surprised when I found out what we was gonna be doin'. But I had already tried workin' in an office and a factory. And I needed to be doin' *somethin'*, so I figger, why not give it a try?

Felisa Santana was already enrolled in classes at the bilingual alternative school when she learned that she was eligible for a part-time CETA job. Her family was having a difficult time making ends meet, and she welcomed the opportunity to earn some money while she was in school. She was also eager to get work experience because she knew that she had to find a full-time job as soon as she completed her GED program. But Felisa had not given much thought to the kind of work she wanted to do. There was an opening for a clerical aid at a neighborhood health clinic near the school, and Felisa's counselor set up an interview for her. Felisa liked the woman who interviewed her, and she felt comfortable at the clinic, which had a bilingual staff and served mostly Hispanics. The CETA job was easy to get to, and since it offered an opportunity to try out clerical work, Felisa decided to give it a try.

The CETA project that Luanne Clawson and Bobby Jones joined provided both GED instruction and part-time work experience. Project participants attended classes in the morning and worked in the community center during the afternoon. Three types of jobs were available: clerical aide, janitorial aide, and social service aide, which meant assisting in the community center's daycare, senior citizens', or recreational programs.

Luanne knew what job she wanted right away. She was interested in secretarial work. She had already taken a course in typing and office practices at West Roxbury High School, and she was ready to try out her skills in a clerical aide position.

Finding a work assignment for Bobby was more difficult. When he was recruited by John Henry, the project director, Bobby said he was ready to get involved in *something*. He was willing to attend classes and he wanted to work. But Bobby was not enthusiastic about any of the jobs the project had to offer:

> John seen me just hangin' 'round the community center, and I guess he figger I was wastin' my life. He told me about this program here and sort of *urged* me to join up. I knew I had to do *somethin'*, to better myself and get me a little education, you know? This was real close to home, and I knew John and everything, so I went ahead and did it.
>
> When it come down to the job—I don't know. I mean, I *wanted* to work and everything, but the jobs they had didn't sound too good. I never liked workin' with my hands, you know? I never saw myself being a janitor, and I couldn't see typin' or secretary stuff. I tried out the daycare for awhile, and I didn't like that too good. So I tol' John I wanted somethin' more inneresting, and he asked me what was I innerested *in*? And I said "Sports," 'cause that's my main thing. So we worked out this job where I would go to all the games and events at the community center and then write up a little somethin' about 'em for the newspaper here.

The young people from Kalamazoo received their CETA job assignments through a consolidated program agency. Carrie Green and Jack Thrush were between jobs when friends told them about the youth program agency, operated by the Kalamazoo Valley Intermediate School District. Carmeletta was looking for her first job. She knew about the agency from her earlier stint in the CETA summer program, and she thought that someone there might be able to help her find a job. All three of these young people wanted full-time work; they were not particularly interested in training or educational services.

Carmeletta had no idea what kind of work she wanted to do, but she asked for a program assignment that could work into a "real" job. Her counselor knew of an open work-experience slot in a state-operated hospital in Kalamazoo. She told Carmeletta that the hospital had hired several young people who had completed their CETA work experiences as orderlies, and she suggested that Carmeletta interview for the position. Carmeletta went to the hospital for the interview, and she decided to take the job:

> I didn't have no trouble gettin' there on the bus or anything, and it looked like a pretty good place to work, you know? The man who interviewed me said they needed someone in the cafeteria to help with the meals and all. I didn't really care *where* I worked that much. I would get minimum wage, he said, while I was in the CETA program. After that there was a chance that I could get hired-on permanent, and then I would be makin' more. He told me about the medical benefits and all. It sounded pretty good, so I decided, you know, that I would take it.

Jack Thrush said he was surprised to find out that he could get a job through the CETA program at the Kalamazoo youth agency. He did not really care what kind of work they gave him, but he thought he might get assigned to a job more quickly if he stated a preference:

> I had a little bit of experience in janitorial work, so that's more or less what I told 'em I'd like to do. The first interview they could line up for me was a maintenance job at the senior citizen's center. I went to the interview the same day, and they said I could have the job.

Carrie did not know what kind of job assignment to request. The youth program counselor who interviewed Carrie told her about a project at the college which provided clerical training, work experience, and counseling for young people who had not yet made vocational plans. Carrie was not sure what that meant, but working at the college sounded a lot better than a job in a factory or restaurant kitchen, and she decided to take the assignment.

Sandy Bonds heard about the CETA program from a young woman she met on the street soon after coming to Portland. When she walked into the Southeast youth service center, she had no idea what to expect:

> Me and my friend, Chris, had just come to Portland. We were livin' more or less on the street and had no money. I met this girl. I didn't know anything about her at all—she was just a stranger on the street, really. But we started talkin', and I told her we needed a place to work. She suggested we go to CETA. She said it was really a great deal and they do a lot of good things.
>
> We went there and filled out these papers. And we were real shocked when the guy there said he did have some jobs, but first he wanted to find out more about what kinds of things we wanted to

do with our lives. I was just thinkin' about any kind of work at all—I just wanted to get a job and make some money, you know? But I started to realize that I could maybe get a better experience than that here—somethin' more dependable—somethin' I could build around for the future.

Sandy and the other young people who came into Portland's Southeast center looking for work were not given immediate job assignments. They attended individual counseling sessions and career research workshops that helped them to define their employment and training needs and consider career alternatives before being assigned to vocational training, GED instruction, work-experience positions, or special CETA projects. During this assessment and research process, Sandy decided that she wanted to do manual work. She wanted an active job, she did not want to spend time sitting at a desk. Carpentry or construction work appealed to Sandy, and she wanted to learn vocational skills on the job, rather than in a classroom. Two weeks after enrolling in the CETA program, Sandy was assigned to a full-time construction and home repair project, located in Southwest Portland and operated by Portland public schools.

Peggy Bromfield was referred to the Southeast center by her AFDC caseworker. She had recently completed a GED program and was interested in getting vocational training. Peggy said the career research workshops at the center helped her to choose a CETA program assignment:

> In career research, we took these tests that CETA gives you. They run 'em through the computer, and you get to see what you're likely to be good at—what you like and what you don't like, you know? We picked out a couple things that the computer said we were good at and that we also thought we were interested in, and we did some research on 'em. I like to work with people, and I'm good with my hands, you know? So I picked beautician and physical therapist. We went out and talked to schools and employers —people in the field—like we were tryin' to get a job. That way we found out as much about it as we could before deciding our training. After doin' the research, I decided I was mostly interested in physical therapy, and I got in the CETA medical careers project at the university hospital.

Tien Van Chin wanted to develop vocational skills that would give him the chance to compete for better jobs. His counselor at the Southeast center suggested that Tien enroll in high school; he could work part-time for a year while he improved his English skills and earned a diploma. But Tien thought that a year in high school would not improve his job prospects much, and he wanted to move more quickly. Tien did some research on the employment outlook for accountants and computer programmers. He found a private business school in Portland that offered a three-semester course in bookkeeping and computer programming. They were willing to accept him without a high school diploma, and Tien's counselor told him that the CETA program would pay his tuition and provide a stipend as long as he maintained passing grades in the business school program.

Douglas Giscard and Jean Ansel were both looking for interesting work with some kind of career future when they enrolled in the CETA program at the Southeast center. Douglas was referred to the program by his juvenile probation officer. Jean heard about the program through a drug rehabilitation counselor. Both of these young people felt they would eventually need to go to college to qualify for the careers they had in mind. But, meanwhile, they needed income to support themselves and the work experience that would help them to settle on specific career objectives.

Douglas had a lot of confidence in his abilities. He expected to earn a lot of money and he could see himself functioning in some kind of professional or managerial position one day. He did his career research on business management, but his CETA counselor told him that the program did not offer work experience in the private sector and he would need a GED and more work experience before he could qualify for one of the few on-the-job training assignments in a private business. Douglas decided to enroll in a GED program, and he set up his own work experience as a staff aide at the Street Shelter, a nonprofit service agency for runaways and other teen-agers out on their own.

Jean knew what kind of work she wanted, but she had no idea how she could get started. Jean had learned how to "sign" for the deaf from a friend when she was still in junior high school. She wanted to work with handicapped children, and she thought her signing skills might be useful. But, as a seventeen-year-old, ninth-grade dropout and rehabilitated heroin addict, Jean did not see herself as a likely candidate for a job in this field. While she was participating in the career research workshop, Jean visited a new public school facility in Portland that had been established to provide educational services for handicapped children. Teachers had been hired for the program, but few had the skills to communicate with deaf pupils. Jean did not meet the school's qualifications for a regular teacher's aide position. But, at the request of her CETA counselor, school officials were more than willing to take on a "free" work experience trainee who knew how to sign.

Jean was elated when she realized that the job she wanted was hers:

You can't imagine how excited I was! It was great to be able to tell my family and friends, "I'm *really* working now!" I could hardly believe they would give me the chance to do this kind of job. Some of my friends had high school diplomas, and they weren't even working at all. Here I had dropped out of school and had so many problems and I had been able to get this really good opportunity. But I was proud of myself, too, 'cause I knew that I had done something to make it happen.

Though not all of the young people in our group were as excited about their assignments as Jean, most of them did view their enrollment in CETA program activities as an event of some significance in their lives. For some it represented an initiation into the working world or a first step back into the mainstream, though these teenagers worried about whether they would be able to fit into a new setting and meet new expectations. As Sandy Bonds said: "I had said I *would* do it, and I was glad about that, but still I was nervous about whether I really *could* do it." Others in the group viewed their program assignments as an opportunity to move out of the world of dead-end jobs into the realm of possible careers. Even those who saw their assignments as "another job" were not inclined to be blasé; they were apt to view the chance for steady work at minimum wage as a step up the employment ladder.

Whatever their expectations or reservations, all of the young people in our group began their program assignments with the intention of doing well and the hope of improving their employment prospects. In the chapters that follow, we will see how they fared as CETA participants, what they learned in their program assignments, and what effects they thought these experiences would have on their lives and employment outlook.

6. Earning and Learning

Getting My Act Together

> When I first started in, you know, just gettin' here every morning
> was a real big thing. I like to stay up late, and it was a long time
> since I had to get myself together—be somewhere ready to go this
> early in the morning, you know? I guess you could say my life
> wasn't exactly set up for it.   *Bobby Jones*

Bobby was not the only young person in our group who had a hard
time conforming to the daily regimen of the classroom or worksite. Program
participation required some changes in life-style, particularly for those
teen-agers who had spent several years out of school and out of the labor
force. Many of the young people I interviewed said they had found the
adjustment to be difficult. Motivation and performance problems were
most apt to arise during the early weeks of program participation. As
Bobby said, "It took me a little time to get my act together."

Sandy Bonds saw herself as a "free person." She was used to an un-
structured life on the road or on the street, and she admits that her life-style
and attitudes caused problems when she first started working at the CETA
home repair project:

> I had problems just getting there at first. I wasn't used to it at all,
> and I was absent a lot in the beginning. It kinda reminded me of
> school, where you *had* to get up and be there every day, and that
> made me not want to go. Also I was a little screwed up physically.
> I'm somewhat of a diabetic, and I hadn't been eating right at all. I'd
> been eating mostly popcorn and potato chips—stuff like that—and
> I was feelin' tired all the time. When I first started workin' I'd be
> late a lot, or when I stayed home, I wouldn't bother callin' in to
> explain.
>
> I got in a lot of trouble about that, you know? They put me
> on probation for a month because of my performance. They told
> me, "If you come in late or don't show up, you're fired!" And then
> I realized, you know, "If you keep messin' up, dummy, you're not
> gonna have a paycheck or a place to live!" Since that time I've had
> almost a perfect record. I've probably put in more hours than

anybody else there. And the more I worked, the more I liked it.

Jean Ansel also went through a difficult adjustment period. Despite her initial elation over her CETA job assignment at the school for handicapped children, Jean found her new work environment intimidating. Her discomfort was reflected in her performance during the first few weeks on the job. But, like Sandy, she was able to weather this period, and the rewards of working were reinforcing:

> It was really hard at first to get myself up and get going each day. There were mornings when I felt like I just couldn't do it, and I wouldn't go in or even call. I'd never thought of havin' a job like this one. I felt like everybody there knew more than I did. And I worried about how I looked—I didn't have too many clothes, and I felt I couldn't wear Levis there, you know? But the work was just so exciting for me—that's really what kept me comin'. And after a while, I got more comfortable with it. When I got some money finally, I was able to go out and buy a few clothes, and my appearance improved. The beginning was definitely the hardest. I thought about quitting and everything. But I got so I didn't want to *ever* quit. After a while, I wouldn't miss work for anything!

The young people who had worked only sporadically, in odd jobs, or on a part-time basis before enrolling in CETA programs were usually eager to begin full-time job assignments; but they were not always prepared to meet the time and energy demands of stable employment. Jack Thrush was pleased with his CETA assignment as a janitorial aide at a senior citizen's center in Kalamazoo. It offered him thirty-five hours of work each week at minimum wage, and he liked the idea of settling into what he viewed as a "more regular" job. But he soon discovered drawbacks:

> At first I was there every day—on time every morning and workin' real hard. But then it started getting to me, you know? Workin' seven hours a day, five days a week didn't leave me no time to socialize at all. The people there were pretty nice, you know, but everyone was busy with their own job, and I was mostly workin' on my own. I got tired of comin' every day, day in and day out, so I started takin' a day off every once in a while to see my friends and stuff like that. I wouldn't get paid for the days I wasn't there, but, apart from that, nobody said too much about it.

The young mothers in our group had a particularly difficult time handling full-time program assignments. Arranging their lives to coordinate childcare and other household responsibilities with new work schedules was a major challenge. Carmeletta DeVries had been a mother for only eight months when she started her CETA job in a Kalamazoo hospital, and there did not seem to be enough hours in the day to get everything done:

> I thought I had it covered pretty good, 'cause my sister said she'd take my baby while I was workin'. But things kept comin' up, you know? And I'd be missin' work, comin' in late, goin' home early, and stuff like that. Like, I wouldn't go in when I had to take my baby to the doctor. You know, they only have certain appointment times at the clinic and you can't get right in there—sometimes you have to wait a long time. Then a couple times, I had to go and get my food stamps. There was always somethin'! Like sometimes I would need to go to the store, and I wouldn't have no money or no food stamps. I wouldn't get out of work till five o'clock and the bank closes at five, so I'd have to leave work early.

Genetta Burke also had a hard time arranging her family life so that she could work thirty-five hours a week on the weatherization project. She had reservations about putting her two preschool-aged children in a daycare program. But the children adjusted well to the new situation, and Genetta believed that the change was good for all of them:

> I was sittin' around the house all day, watchin' soap operas on TV, and I knew that *I* had to get out and do somethin'. But I wasn't too happy about puttin' my kids out with strangers, you know? Before when I worked, my grandma watched my little boy, but she was gettin' to where she was just too old to handle 'em, so I decided to try it out with this daycare over at Victoria Point. It worked out good, too. I just take 'em with me in the mornin' and drop 'em off. It was a lot better than I thought, 'specially for my daughter. She been kinda shy and scared of other kids, but she got to where she was wantin' to go there every day. Even on weekends and stuff, she'd be sayin', "Scoo, Mommy? Nettie go scoo?" And my son, he be runnin' around there, actin' like he own the place. Gettin' out of the house, you know, it turned out to be a good thing for all of us.

Setting up a life-style that sustains a work regimen is a key step in employability development. Many young people need help to make this adjustment. The responsiveness of program counselors and work supervisors in recognizing special needs and circumstances and helping to set guidelines seemed to be an important factor in program success or failure for the young people in our group. Carmeletta never discussed her scheduling problems with her supervisor. She continued to miss work and eventually lost her CETA job. Jack Thrush was also to leave his job without discussing or resolving his problems.

Peggy Bromfield's difficulties as a single parent were compounded by a drinking problem. With the help of her supervisor, though, Peggy was able to work out her problems and continue with her assignment in the medical careers project:

> I was still drinkin' heavy when I first started workin'. I'd turn off the alarm automatically in the morning, and then I wouldn't go in. I wouldn't even call up. I felt bad about it, you know? But I was ashamed to tell my supervisor, Lila. I thought, if you got bad personal problems, you shouldn't be workin' at a hospital. But finally, I had to tell her, and she was pretty understanding. She asked me if I thought I could stop, and we talked about how to do it. Then I took off work for a week and quit drinkin'.
>
> Then right after that, the kids got the measles and I couldn't find anyone to watch them. I found out about it at work, and I started crying 'cause I knew I was gonna have to stay home. Lila talked to me about it. She said, "Don't worry, we'll let you make up the time, and you won't lose any pay." I said, "I'm more worried about losing the experience." I was causing problems for everyone, and I thought maybe I shouldn't be workin' at all. But she said, "Peggy, things like this happen to every woman with kids. You'll get through it okay." And I did. I came back a week later, and after that things started to work out much better.

What It Means to Work

> I feel really good about things—about myself and what I've done here. When I first started, I had no idea what they expected of me. I had no idea *what* to expect, really. It was a whole new world. But I feel that bein' here has changed me. I learned to do the work, start new things, follow through with 'em. I've accomplished a lot, and I feel satisfied that I've done a good job.   *Felisa Santana*

Most of the young people in our group were expected to do more than merely show up on time, dress appropriately, and observe the protocol of the workplace. They were given specific job assignments and were expected to earn the income provided to them by the CETA program. For some of the teen-agers I interviewed, program participation provided the first opportunity to experience the sense of accomplishment that comes from hard work and a job well done. Those, like Felisa, who were kept busy and given the chance to learn new things were most apt to be happy with their job assignments and to be satisfied with their own performance.

The ability to work—i.e., to take direction, cooperate with others, exert the self-discipline, and expend the energy required to follow a task through to completion—is a prerequisite to employability. Most youth program planners and administrators believe that a thorough understanding of what it means to work is more important than the development of specific vocational skills. The majority of new entrants to America's workforce learn their occupational skills on the job.

Some participants in youth employment programs are placed directly in unsubsidized jobs or assigned to on-the-job-training positions in the private sector. Others, like Felisa, are assigned to subsidized entry-level jobs in public or private nonprofit agencies. But young people who lack experience, and who have difficulty communicating with others and applying themselves to assigned tasks, do not fit easily into regular work environments. If placed on their own in even an entry-level work situation, they face a high probability of failure.

Community improvement projects, such as the Victoria Point weatherization project, offer an alternative to individual work-experience assignments. These projects are required, by law, to provide a service or product of tangible benefit to the community. The young people who participate are given a chance to earn an income and develop basic work skills in a sheltered environment while contributing to the welfare of their community. Project participants work in groups—typically, five to ten teen-agers work together—under the supervision of one adult crew leader. Most of the work is physical labor. No previous experience is required, and necessary skills are taught on the job or at the project facility. Most community improvement projects are designed to be completed within twelve months. While young people may spend a full year in project jobs, they are expected to move on to more challenging jobs, school programs, or work-experience assignments.

Some of the results of community improvement projects are apparent: weatherized homes in low-income neighborhoods, public lands cleared of weeds and debris, renovated buildings, refurbished parks, and new trails and bicycle paths. But how well do the projects work for the young people who participate? What do they learn about the meaning of work?

In addition to his work on the weatherization project, Adam Sledge worked nights as a security aide in the Victoria Point housing project under a special crime-prevention program, but he had never held an unsubsidized job. While Adam knew his wages were being paid by the CETA program, he viewed himself as a worker, not as a program participant, and he thought the work environment and requirements of the weatherization project were probably much like those of any job:

I picked this job in the first place 'cause it was right in the [housing] project and all. But as far as I can see it's about what you find on any other job. I been here 'bout five months now, and I like the work. We do stuff like insulate walls and ceilin's, wrap the pipes and water heaters, weather-strippin', fix up busted doors and windows—stuff like that. It's pretty easy for me, you know, 'cause I'm used to workin' with my hands. I fixed the ceilin's in my mother's place, paint the apartment up, and all that by myself, so most of what we do on this job, I picked up real quick, you know?

Way we do it here, we work five or six of us on a crew. They drive us out to the house, tell us what to do, and we go to work on it. It works out pretty good. Most of the time we keep busy. 'Course sometimes, they run out of materials, or they don't have the work lined up, or the van's out or somethin', and then we just hangin' out, waitin' 'round, you know? Some people on the crew, they like to fool around, but I'd say we mostly work pretty hard.

Adam's supervisor told me that he was one of the best workers on his weatherization crew. Moreover, Adam's experience on the project encouraged higher aspirations:

I like workin' here okay, but I still keep my eyes open, you know, for another job? I'd like to be makin' more than what I get here. I hear where some of those jobs in construction pay like ten, twelve dollars an hour—I'd like to get somethin' like that, you know? If I don't run into somethin' better, I'll just stay here, you know, 'til this job ends. I'll get the experience here and then move on up to somethin' else.

Though Adam was working and performing well on the weatherization project, his belief that twelve months of experience on the project crew would qualify him for a high-paying job in the construction industry was not very realistic. He knew little about actual opportunities or requirements in this field; his expectations were based solely on his project experience. Adam's gauged his own capabilities by assessing the requirements of his project job—which was composed largely of simple, repetitive tasks —and by comparing the quality of his work to that of the other members of his crew, most of whom were less industrious and less skilled than he. The two other young people in our group who were on the weatherization project were less impressed than Adam with the quality of work experience they were receiving.

Though Genetta Burke knew virtually nothing about weatherization or repair work when she came to the project, she had worked before, both in a factory and in an office, and her perspective was different from Adam's. Genetta said:

As far as the basic skills of the job went—I gotta hand it to 'em—they did a pretty good job of teachin' us. I didn't know how to use the tools, measure out the stuff, or any of that, but they took the time to show us, and they had a lot of patience, which made it easier, you know?

But I don't think much about the way the work crews are set up. The guys in this project are just too young. They don't know anything about work, and they play too much. They gang around, tell jokes, and stuff like that when we s'posed to be workin'. Sometimes they fool around all day. Sometimes, I feel like this job is a joke. I come here if I wanna laugh, you know?

It's hard to take this job serious. Most the time, the staff treat us like babies. They got all these rules, you know, and you gotta do everything with your crew, never on your own. I get tired sometimes of ridin' around in the van with all these kids. Half the time they get lost and can't find where they're goin'. They never tell us what's goin' on ahead of time.

We haffta wait around all the time to find out if we goin' out on a job or what we gonna do that day. You do learn some skills here, you know? But we do the same few things over and over. I don't think it's much like a *real* job.

Genetta needed more experience and better work skills to compete successfully in the labor force. But her needs were special, and, as the mother of two children and the head of her own household, she was too mature to be a good candidate for a community improvement project. Genetta enrolled in the weatherization project because it offered a steady income without jeopardizing her welfare benefits, and she had "nothing better to do." Though she soon found the work offered little challenge and held no career interest for her, she continued her participation in the project until it ended:

I thought about quittin' a few times, but where was I gonna go? I like earnin' some extra money, and gettin' out and goin' to work every day. This job ain't too bad, when the houses we go to are nice and clean, you know? 'Course most of the people's houses we been workin' on ain't clean at all. I don't really *like* workin' in places like that, but they take me out on those jobs anyway.

If they ain't pushin' me too much, it's okay. Like yesterday, they had me weatherstrippin' a door. I like to do *that*. But then they wanted me to paint the door and all the basement windows at the same time. Now that made me mad. I just told 'em I wasn't doin' all that. I'd weatherstrip the doors and windows, but forget all this paintin' and stuff!

I don't want to make a career outta this kinda work or nothin'.

Only way I'd work in weatherizin' is if I couldn't think of another trade, or if there was nothin' else left. I guess I would do it *then,* you know? But sayin', like, am I gonna jump right into it? No. Still, I guess it's good I learned how to do it so, you know, I have some kinda skill aside if some other kind of trainin' don't work out for me.

Harold Thomas viewed his job on the weatherization project as a stopgap—a way to earn some money while he studied for his GED and got ready to enlist in the army. He spent five months in the project and does not think that it taught him much about working:

The actual job ain't too bad, you know? I mean the work itself is simple—you can learn to do it fast—it don't require much skill at all. I didn't mind it when we *was* workin' you know. The main thing wrong with it was that we spent too much time just waitin' around. We had'ta wait a couple weeks in the beginnin' for them to get the jobs lined up. Then once we got goin', you know, they was always runnin' out of materials and stuff. Some of the people was there to work, but there was some of them never did learn to do the job right. I stuck it out 'cause I needed the money. I was just there temporary anyway—couldn't see no future in it, you know?

Sven Latoka had previous work experience when he signed up for a community improvement project in Jamaica Plain, but he still found his job on a renovation crew to be a worthwhile experience. Though Sven also reported that work was sometimes held up when his crew ran out of materials or had to wait for another crew to finish their part of a job, he said that he didn't spend much time just sitting around:

I've been busy myself. You know, it's up to the individual, really. If you want to keep yourself busy, you can. Some people are just lazy. If there's nothin' else to do, you can always pick up a broom, clear away the trash—stuff like that. You know, on any construction job, there's just certain things that come up—not everybody can work all the time with no delays or anything— that's just the way this business is.

With the training he got from his father and his experience in carpentry, Sven was considerably more skilled than the other young people working with him on the renovation project. After observing Sven's work during his early weeks on the job, his crew supervisor talked to the project director, and they decided to make use of Sven's skills and give him more responsibilities. Though his wages and official status remained unchanged, Sven was given the opportunity to function as a work crew supervisor. In this role, he provided training and directed the work of other participants as well as consulting with project staff on work plans and schedules. Sven stayed with the renovation project for nine months, and as the end of his time there drew near, he said:

> I like most things about this project. I wasn't too sure in the beginning, but I gotta say that it's been a good experience for me. I learned some new things here. With my dad, it was mostly small remodel jobs, you know? But here we're doin' what you'd call more of a *major* renovation on public buildings. I've learned how to tear down and put up inside walls, how to work from blueprints, and stuff like that. I've also learned a lot more about how to estimate materials and figure time and labor for different kinds of jobs. I expect to do regular construction work when I get through here, and those things are gonna help me a lot.

Sandy Bonds had no construction skills and little experience with work of any sort when she enrolled in a construction and home repair project operated by the Portland public school system. Though project crews worked on public buildings and in low-income neighborhoods as well as at the training site, the project was not designed primarily with community improvement in mind. Its major purpose was to provide its participants with basic training and work experience in a variety of construction, installation, and building-repair capacities. After five months on the project Sandy was enthusiastic about what she was learning:

> This is the first real job I've had, and I like it a lot. Right now I'm workin' sheetrock and concrete. I've also worked linoleum, formica, and roofing. They have five crews here who do general carpentry. One crew does mostly roofing. Another does mostly little things, like puttin' guard rails in an elderly person's home, adjustin' the house for them so they can get around better, you know? I'll probably get a chance to try out everything before I'm done here. I think it's great. I learn so much every day! It kind of gives me a sense of responsibility, when someone says, "Go do this," and I can do it!

The Dorchester CETA project in which Luanne Clawson and Bobby Jones were enrolled was designed to provide an orientation to work and a chance to develop good work habits and basic skills in a sheltered environment. Participants were given part-time jobs under the supervision of community center staff rather than being assigned to full-time work crews.

Working in an office was a novel experience for Luanne. But the clerical staff in the community center's administrative office were willing to show her the ropes, and the woman who supervised Luanne encouraged her to take on new tasks as she became ready. Five months after she began work, Luanne said she was pleased with the variety in her job and satisfied with her own performance:

> I like this job very, very much. I don't think you could ever get bored with it. You know, there's different things to be doin' all the time. 'Bout the first thing I learned was handlin' the phones —you know, takin' down messages and puttin' calls through and stuff? I'm good at that, and I still do it sometimes. But more and more, they been givin' me typin' work. I type memos, announcements—even letters. I'm not real fast yet, but I do a good job on it. And I run the xerox machine, sort mail, you know, and take it 'round to people's desks and stuff. I like most everything 'bout this job, and I'm doin' good work here too. Mrs. Jackson—she's my supervisor, you know—she say she can really *depend* on me. With what I'm doin' here, I think I learn way more 'bout bein' a secretary than what I could pick up, you know, in school or any place like that.

Luanne reported to the same office each afternoon. Her responsibilities were clearly defined, and she received a good deal of training and support from her supervisor. In his special assignment as a sports reporter for the community center newspaper, Bobby Jones had no specified work station, and he was allowed to move freely about the community center. He was supposed to report directly to John Henry, the CETA project director. But John was usually busy with other things, and Bobby received little training or supervision.

While he attended most of the games and enjoyed playing the role of a reporter, Bobby had a difficult time getting his reports down on paper. Few stories were actually submitted to the paper, and Bobby spent many of his afternoons wandering around the community center watching other people work. Though he admits to not working much, Bobby thinks he learned a lot about what it means to work from observing others. And he wasn't that impressed with what he saw:

> I been up here at the center a lot, watchin' these people work, you know? It's all different kinds of work goin' on in this building. I know. I ask people how they do it, watch what they do. I know how they work the switchboard upstairs and things like that. You know—bein' up here so much and knowin' all the executive

dudes of the buildin' real good like I do—I get to see a lot.
Mostly, a lot of the jobs they do here have paperwork. I see
where a lot of people get real *mean* from that kind of work. You
know, you can see it—you can just *see* it. They come to work,
and they all tight—tense, you know—*mean*. It shows on 'em—it
shows. Eight hours a day really *get* to them people.

Bobby says his experience at the community center has convinced
him that he could never be happy as an "executive dude." He also has
a prejudice against "social workin' jobs" or any kind of trade where
you "use your hands to make a livin'." Ever since he was a small boy,
Bobby has wanted to be a professional athlete; and nothing in his experience—in or outside the CETA program—has encouraged him to consider other careers.

Fitting into an Organization

Some of the young people in our group had the opportunity to
learn new skills and try out new work roles away from the sheltered environment of the youth program agency or project facility. Felisa
Santana, Carmeletta DeVries, Douglas Giscard, and Jean Ansel were
given individual work-experience assignments in public or private nonprofit agencies. They took on new responsibilities without the bolstering
presence of a program counselor or crew leader. Though their wages
were paid by the CETA program, and their status was that of a trainee
rather than a regular worker, they were faced with the same challenge
confronting any new employee: learning to perform a job and to fit into
an organization. The challenge had special significance for these young
people—they knew that if they could make a place for themselves
within the organization and perform well as a work-experience participants, there would be a chance to be hired as regular workers.

Felisa was nervous about starting her job as a clerical aide at a
neighborhood health clinic in Boston. She knew she would be expected
to work, but she could not envision what she could actually do to earn
her CETA paycheck. She had no clerical skills and no office experience.
Her first days on the job were trying. But her coworkers were willing to
help her out, and things soon got better:

Mrs. Garcia, she was my supervisor. The first day I came to the
job, she took me all 'round the clinic and introduce me to everyone there—the doctors and everything. Then we go back to the
office, you know, and she asked me what kind of work I would
like to start first. I didn't know what to say. I was embarrassed,

you know, 'cause I really couldn't think of anything I could do. I didn't know how to type or nothing, and I had never even worked on a copy machine. Finally, she said, "Well, you know the alphabet, don't you? There are some things you can file." She gave me some bills and records to file. But I had a hard time, you know, even to do *that* at first. It took me a while to catch on to the system. I had to ask the other women working there for help. They was very nice about it—this one woman, Consuela, especially. We got to be good friends later, you know? She said, "It take everybody some time to learn. You can't start right out on your own. There's a trick to everything, you know." They were so nice about showing me things. They had to take time out from whatever they was doing to teach me. And I really wanted to learn, you know, so that I could help out, 'stead of getting in their way all the time. And little by little it got so I could do more things on my own.

Three months after she started her job at the clinic, Felisa signed up for typing and bookkeeping courses at the bilingual school. She attended classes every morning and worked in the afternoons. As her secretarial skills improved, Felisa's job was expanded to include new functions. By the time she passed her GED examinations, Felisa was handling much of the clinic's billing and account work. After working eighteen months as a CETA aide, Felisa was offered, and accepted, a full-time job at the clinic as a billing clerk.

As a CETA trainee, Felisa received special consideration and help from her coworkers at the clinic. But there were other young people I interviewed who felt that their special status as CETA participants set them apart from regular employees in negative, rather than positive, ways. Peggy Bromfield, who worked in a Portland hospital as a participant in a CETA medical careers project, said:

Some of the staff there really helped me, but they look down on you, too, you know? I mean, they introduce you to patients and new staff by saying, "This is Peggy. She's on CETA. I don't know what CETA means, but she's on it." You know, they treat you like you're just temporary help and don't count for much. I was workin' there full-time, you know, and doin' a lot of good. But the regular therapy assistant, Donna, she always took all of the credit.

Carmeletta DeVries spent six months in her CETA job as a food service aide in a Kalamazoo hospital. Though the work was routine, she liked it well enough to hope for a permanent position there. But Carmeletta felt she was discriminated against because she was a CETA participant.

> We would hand out breakfast to the patients, you know, wipe the tables, sweep the floors—everybody would get out and help clean up. Then, later, we would pour the milk for dinner, serve the dinner, then go up on the units and put laundry away. I liked it quite a lot. But, you know, sometimes I was treated different, just 'cause I was a CETA worker. I didn't think that was fair!
>
> There was signs up that said, "Don't let CETA workers use your keys," or "CETA workers cannot answer or use the telephone." God! I felt I was treated like a patient or somethin'. You know: "Don't let patients or CETA workers. . . ." I couldn't use anyone's keys, and the simple fact was that everywhere you go there's a lock. When I got ready to leave, I might have only a minute or two to get across the street to the bus stop. But I'd haffta run all the way back to the cafeteria to get somebody to unlock the door for me. I didn't think that was right!
>
> And then, there was the windows they had me washin'! They were these big cafeteria windows that they don't wash but every year or so, you know? They said, "You're a CETA worker, and all the CETA workers have to wash the windows." And I say, "If I wasn't here, who'd wash these windows?" I was really mad, you know? Here people was sittin' around on their coffee breaks. I'm up there washin' the windows like some monkey, while everybody else sittin' 'round talkin'. I didn't think that was fair!

Douglas Giscard didn't feel that his CETA status triggered any discrimination in his job at the Street Shelter. This nonprofit Portland agency, which provided counseling and emergency services to runaways and "street kids," was funded through private contributions and small public grants. Apart from the director, two counselors, and a part-time secretary, the Street Shelter depended on the help of teen-aged and adult volunteers. As a CETA participant, Douglas was the only teenager who worked full-time at the agency and was paid for his services. When he started out at the Street Shelter, Douglas's role was not clearly defined; and he discovered that he could expand his job functions to fit his own abilities and the needs of the agency:

> I believe my official title was office aide, but nobody was too clear about what that involved. The director told me that the counseling staff could use some clerical support—answering the phones, greeting people when they came in the office, keeping track of appointments, and stuff like that—especially on the days when the secretary wasn't there. That was fine with me. I did

whatever they asked—and I kept my eyes open for other things to do, you know?

I would talk to the counselors and find out what they needed. They would be tied up a lot of the time with clients. And while they were in their offices in session with the clients, there'd be all these kids, milling around, asking questions, and tryin' to figure out what they were supposed to do. It was pretty clear that they needed help directing the volunteers and coordinating the different services they were involved in. So I got in the habit, you know, of sitting down with the counselors each morning and laying out what needed to be done. Then I'd draw up a schedule of activities and make up a sign-up sheet for volunteers. After a few months, they gave me the title of youth volunteer coordinator.

I've been coordinating the volunteers for about six months now, and I can handle just about anything else that needs to be done around here. I work with the clients, but I don't get involved in the actual counseling, you know. They've pretty much promised me a permanent job. It should come through in a month or two, if they have the funding for it.

When Jean Ansel started her CETA job at a school for handicapped children, she was not sure what her role was supposed to be. At first she found it hard to fit in. But she was eager to work, and her signing skills were in demand at the school. After several weeks of briefings and temporary assignments in different classrooms, Jean was asked to fill the role of teaching assistant. She worked with a classroom of deaf children, under the direction of a special education instructor. While she was working at the school Jean passed her GED examinations and completed two community college courses in rehabilitation and special education. Ten months after Jean began her work experience, there was a job opening at the school. She could hardly believe it when she got the job:

One of the teachers told me that there was a teacher's aide position opening up, and she said that I should apply for it, 'cause then I'd be a permanent school district employee, and I would get better benefits and more money than what I was gettin' in the CETA program. I went ahead and applied, but I didn't think there was much chance that I would actually get the job. I was workin' as an aide already, but the regular aides in this school are like what teachers are in most schools—they do most all of the actual work in the classroom. I knew that there would be people who were applying with college degrees and several years' experience, you know? I couldn't believe it when the vice-principal called me into her office and told me that I had the job! She said, "Jean, you've done an *excellent* job for us so far, and we'd really hate to lose you." That made me feel even more terrific. I was on top of the world!

Exploring Careers

I like to think I *could* make good choices about my own career, but I don't really know that much about what's out there to do. I've learned some things about the workin' world, you know? But not necessarily the things I want. I don't have enough information about the things I want.   *Carrie Green*

Most of the young people in our group were not ready to make career choices when they entered CETA programs. Their previous experience at home, at school, or even at work had given them only a limited understanding of occupational roles, requirements, and possibilities. They needed better preparation and more information before they could make realistic plans for a career. Though the CETA program gave them the chance to earn an income and improve basic work skills, Carrie and some of the others had little opportunity in their CETA jobs to explore potential careers.

But several young people in our group did have the opportunity as CETA participants to observe and practice a variety of occupational skills and try on new career roles. Peggy Bromfield and Sandy Bonds were assigned to CETA projects designed specifically for career exploration.

Peggy was enrolled in a hospital-based medical careers project. In addition to training and work experience in physical therapy, she received career planning information and exposure to a variety of medical occupations:

For six hours every day, I would be workin' with the physical therapists—mostly in the hydro room. The other two hours, we would all get together to meet different people at the hospital and find out about different medical fields—like psychiatrist, speech therapist, physical therapist, midwife, LPN, paramedic instructor, and so on. We got to observe them workin', and they would tell us about what they do, what they get paid, how much schooling is needed, how they got where they are, and what they think the benefits are and what the disadvantages are of their job. It was real good for *me* because—wanting to be a physical therapist—you have to understand what all the other medical fields are about 'cause, you know, you're gonna be workin' with 'em.

Peggy discovered that college or vocational training was a require-
ment for most of the work in the hospital. Certification as a physical
therapy assistant generally requires two years of vocational training in
an accredited program. But, after some introductory training, Peggy was
allowed to assist the therapists in the hydro room as a work-experience
participant. Peggy enjoyed working with the patients; she seemed to
have a gift for physical therapy. As she demonstrated more competence
for the work, her responsibilities in the hydro room were increased and
her confidence grew. But Peggy was not a licensed therapist, and she ran
into problems with her coworkers when she began to try out some of her
own ideas and techniques:

> The people I worked with were really impressed with me at first,
> 'cause I had so much energy. I really wanted to learn and to get
> things done. After a few months in the hydro room, I was workin'
> pretty much as a physical therapist assistant. The girl that was
> trainin' me went off on vacation, and she gave me two weeks to
> prove myself by workin' on my own.
>
> But I ran into problems, you know? 'Cause I *cared* too much
> about the patients. The physical therapist was too busy concen-
> trating on their physical abilities to even bother with their mental
> abilities. So I would talk to the patients a lot, you know? Reas-
> sure them while they were getting therapy and try and distract
> them from the pain.
>
> But the therapist got pissed off about it, and she told my
> project supervisor that I was bein' too friendly with the patients. I
> couldn't see where I was doin' anything wrong, you know? But
> my supervisor said, "Why do you think the therapist would tell
> me these things? Think about it over the weekend and see if you
> can figure out what to do about it."
>
> I was pretty confused, and I didn't think she was bein' really
> straight with me. I mean, why should they care if I wanted to be
> nice and try to help the patients out? When I thought more about
> it, I decided that one thing was they were worried about me
> bein' *too* nice—especially with the men—worried that the
> patients might get the wrong impression. I had made this one guy
> a cake—'cause I felt sorry for him, you know?—and he had
> gotten kind of a crush on me. I knew they didn't like *that*. But I
> also thought they might of been mad 'cause I was doin' half their
> job, and I'm just a CETA trainee, you know?
>
> Well, I finally figured out that I could be a little more pro-
> fessional, you know, and still be friendly and be myself. So I
> acted more the way the therapist wanted, but I still tried to help

the patients understand what they were goin' through and explain the things that were happening to them when they're in the hydro room.

Peggy spent seven months in the medical careers project. She received an intensive exposure to a hospital and had a chance to work as a physical therapy assistant. She reported that her experience in the project helped her to settle on career objectives:

> Going through that experience helped me realize that I really do want to work in physical therapy. I learned a lot from the hospital—some of the staff there really helped me. But I don't think I would like to work in a hospital; it's just too cold and business-like. I think most of 'em are just too busy to really think about *people*. To be a licensed physical therapist, like in a hospital, you need to go to college for four years. I'd like to be a therapy assistant and work with patients at a private clinic or a chiropractor's. That's what I plan to look into next, you know?

The majority of young women who enroll in youth employment programs receive work experience and training in occupational areas that have traditionally employed high percentages of women workers. In service occupations such as clerical work, food service, cosmetology, and so on, job openings are fairly plentiful, and young people can often handle entry-level positions with relatively little advanced training. But traditionally female occupations typically pay considerably less than jobs that have historically been held by men. Youth employment specialists and program counselors are encouraging more young women to prepare for better-paying jobs in male-dominated career fields. What kind of problems does a young woman face when she tries a career that traditionally has been assumed exclusively by men?

When Sandy Bonds signed up for the construction and home repair project in Portland, she had no experience working with tools and knew nothing about basic construction techniques. Sandy is five feet tall and weighs less than 100 pounds. Though she considers herself a feminist, she does not think that she had a need to prove anything by tackling a nontraditional job, and she wasn't motivated by the salary potential in the building trades. She wanted a job that allowed her to move around, use her body, and not be tied to a desk. Construction work seemed a logical choice. But Sandy knew that it would not be easy:

> I took a chance, really, with this project. I was interested in construction work, but I took a chance at the same time. I'm not a big person—or that strong, really. And I had no experience

in this kind of work. I realized, you know, that some people get
carried away with themselves and start testin' the people around
them. I don't like gettin' involved in these little games—these
trips around, "I'm bigger than you are and stronger than you
are"—that just bothers me. I don't know why people want to do
that anyway—there's no reason for it. If he's a man, he's a man. If
she's a woman, she's a woman. You don't have to prove that to
anyone, we already know that. A lot of people feel they have to
prove themselves, but there's really no reason to do that. Still, I
had'ta admit that there was a lot I needed to learn, and I didn't
expect it to be that easy, you know?

Sandy found there was even more to learn than she had expected.
The adjustment period was difficult for her, but she feels that her instructors did a good job:

It was pretty confusing at first. The work, itself, is not so hard,
but learnin' how to do it right is what's hard. I doubt if you could
pick anybody up off the street and ask 'em to hammer a nail and
they would do it right—without bendin' the nail or anything.
There's a little technique to everything we learned.
   The first instructor I had was a woman. She was kinda new to
the whole thing, and she was kinda learnin' along with us. She
was a good instructor, though. The second was an older man who
had been in construction for years, and he was really super good.
He had us do classwork. We were the only crew that did it, 'cause
he wanted us to learn vocabulary. Because, like, we would be
workin' along, and he would ask somebody to get him a jack
plate. And we'd all turn around and look at him and say, "What's
a jack plate?" So finally, he said, "Look, I'm makin' this
vocabulary list for you. This is what you've got to learn to do the
job. You have to know what things are first, that's pretty clear."
So that's what he did, and it turned out to be real good.

After Sandy had been at the construction and home repair project
for about five months, she was placed on a new crew to learn cabinetry
and finish work. Though she had a particular interest in this aspect of
carpentry, Sandy had trouble with the crew assignment. The crew leader
did not like the idea of women working on a construction site, and he
gave the two young women on his crew a hard time. Sandy disliked his
approach. She thought his attitude made it harder to learn, but she was
determined to do a good job on his crew all the same:

He's one of those guys who thinks you gotta be tough and rough
in the construction business—so he's gonna give the women on

his crew a hard time, you know? He said we gotta learn that we're gonna be hassled on the job—one of those little philosophies! I don't agree with his approach at all. I think he's just playin' games, myself. A thirty-five-year-old man, playin' games on teen-age girls? Some instructor!

I don't like offending people at all, you know? I try not to. But I don't like holdin' myself back to fit somebody's ideas about me either. So if I have to prove somethin', I usually try to do it in the nicest way I can. I'm not tryin' to *prove* anything by bein' here, you know? But if he wants to see it like that, fine. If it's a matter of doin' good work, that's fine too. I know I can do it, and I'll show it to him.

Though Sandy worked hard on the cabinetry crew, she continued to have problems with her crew leader. The other young woman on the crew became discouraged and dropped out of the project; but Sandy did not want to jeopardize, or be driven out of, her project job, and she finally asked the supervisor for a new crew assignment. Though she was not happy about giving up the opportunity to learn more about finish work, Sandy had developed a philosophical attitude about the problems and prejudice that a woman is bound to encounter in the construction field:

It's not so hard on me, 'cause I can take a lot, you know, and it's what I wanna do. But it's real hard for most women. 'Cause all of a sudden, what's called "femininity" is not there anymore when you try to lift up sixteen feet of two-by-fours or somethin' like that. You've been taught that if you have any muscles in your arm, you're gonna look like a boy—that they're gonna call you a butch and all that stuff. I mean, most women'll freak out on that 'cause they know that society doesn't like it. They're taught that, you know, and it's a shame. It really is, I think.

But men that are gonna stay macho 'cause that's what their dad taught 'em are just as bad off. A man workin' in a feminine job—like a flower salesman or somethin'—he's gonna be defensive too, you know? I feel sorry for the kind of guy who thinks, "This is a macho job, and I'm not gonna give no woman no slack on my construction site!" That's crazy, really. You don't have to dress like you were taught to dress and act just like you were taught to act.

Women have to wear grubby clothes when they work construction, and they have to do heavy work. I think it's hard for most of 'em. Sometimes, you know, it's not that they *get* so much shit on the job; it's more like they *expect* a lot of shit. To some extent, it depends on *who* you are and *how* you act, in terms of how much garbage you actually get from other people on the job. I can see why some women back down all the time 'cause they weren't taught that they *shouldn't* back down. I don't know, it's kinda complicated, you know?

It is complicated. As Sandy pointed out, a young person entering a nontraditional career field faces internal as well as external barriers. Construction work would not be a good choice for many young women, but Sandy feels it was the right choice for her. Her experience on the construction and home repair project has taught her that you can do almost anything if you set your mind to it:

> Some things are harder than others, and you gotta be able to admit it if you need help. Women are afraid to ask men things, but how are you gonna learn if you don't ask? Personally, if I can't do somethin', I just speak up and say I haven't done it before, you know? If that's true, then someone'll usually be glad to show you how to do it.
>
> 'Course you haffta be ready to follow through on your own. Once they show you somethin', you can't be expectin' 'em to do it for you. But, really, there's a trick to everything, and just about anyone can learn it if they really want to. Um, like, see that door sittin' over there? Hollow-core door, just a piece of veneer plywood in it, right? It wouldn't weigh more'n about twenty-five pounds. But it's real big and wide, and you wonder how somebody my size could carry it, you know, without hurtin' themselves. Well, I've learned how to carry things without killin' myself, you know?
>
> It's simple, really. Most things that are heavy, if you know how to balance 'em with your weight, then you can pick 'em up. I stacked four ten-foot pressure-treated two-by-fours on my shoulder this morning. It was maybe seventy pounds of wood. But if you just stick it up on your shoulder and have the weight towards the back and hold the front end with your arm to balance it, there's just no problem. You know, the legs on a person are awful powerful! When you lift, you use your legs anyway, not your back. Once you learn how to pick things up, there's no problem. And you can learn anything like that. Just depends on what you want.

Vocational Credentials

Some young people already know what they want when they enter employment and training programs. Todd Clinton had decided to become a hairstylist before he came to Portland's Southeast youth service center. This was not a tentative choice. He had already had an opportunity to learn basic work skills and experiment with a variety of occupational roles.

Five years of work experience in his father's business had convinced Todd that he did not want a future in fiberglass construction. During his three semesters at the school district skills center, he had developed skills and discovered his aptitude for design work. While in the National Guard he had considered a career in radio, but his brief training did not encourage him to be optimistic about his prospects as a disc jockey. Todd had done his own research on the hair design industry. He had discovered that vocational training and state certification were required to qualify for entry-level work as a hairstylist. He knew it was a competitive field, characterized by low pay and high turnover in most entry-level jobs and by uncertain prospects for advancement. But Todd felt he had a talent for design, and he believed he could be successful in the hair design industry.

Very few teen-agers enter employment and training programs with as much work experience, vocational training, and career exposure behind them as Todd. Tien Van Chin, like most of the other young people in our group, was not ready to make a final career choice. But several years of experience in the unskilled labor market had given Tien the discipline and incentive to move on to more challenging and rewarding work. His long-range goal was a university education; but to achieve this, he needed to improve his immediate employment prospects. He was ready to settle on an interim occupation, and he wanted vocational training and credentials that would qualify him for better employment opportunities. Several weeks of career research as a CETA participant convinced Tien that business school education and a certificate in computer programming and book-keeping would give him a competitive edge.

Youth employment and training agencies are allowed to use federal program funds to purchase tuition and provide stipends for young people enrolled in accredited vocational education programs at public schools or private institutions such as the Belle Vista Hair Design Academy or the Portland business college that Tien selected. But youth program sponsors tend to use this approach sparingly. It is generally expensive in comparison to other service options, and students may require up to two years of support before they can qualify for vocational certification.

Teen-agers who have dropped out of high school, have accrued little work experience, and have limited knowledge of career alternatives are not usually considered good risks for individual vocational education subsidies. Successful completion of a vocational certification program requires motivation, self-discipline, and basic academic skills. Most program sponsors do not want to risk limited training dollars on young people who are not ready. Todd and Tien were able to convince their CETA counselors at Portland's Southeast center that they were good risks. How did they fare in the vocational education programs they selected?

After two years of menial work Tien was eager to be a student again. He was confident of his academic abilities and study skills. He had done well at the private lyceum in Saigon, where he had gone to school until he was fourteen. In addition to Chinese and his native Vietnamese language, Tien spoke some French. But he had no formal English instruction until he reached the refugee camp in Thailand. He learned enough English at the camp for rudimentary communication, and his conversational skills improved when he reached Portland and began working. But Tien lacked the English vocabulary and writing facility to compete well in an academic or technical environment. Though the concepts presented in the coursework on accounting, statistics, computer language, and programming techniques were not hard for Tien to grasp, he had difficulty understanding his instructors, especially when they spoke too quickly, and it was hard for him to phrase questions and communicate his own ideas in the classroom.

His first term at the business college was the most difficult. He had to drop one class and struggled to get a "C" average in the others. At the beginning of the second term his CETA counselor met with Tien and his advisor from the business school to evaluate his progress in the program and reconsider his enrollment. The CETA counselor was concerned that Tien's English deficiencies might be a serious barrier to his successful completion of the program. But the business school advisor felt that Tien was doing reasonably well, and Tien, himself, reported that he had formed a study group with other students in the program and that the social interaction outside the classroom was helping to improve his English.

Tien was allowed to continue in the business school program. During his second term he took a full course-load, and he finished the term with an "A" in one course and "Bs" in the rest. During his third term Tien began practicum work in the school's computer center, and he proved to have facility for programming. His instructors and advisor viewed Tien as a successful student, and they were confident that he would be able to secure a job as a computer programmer when his coursework at the school was completed.

Todd encountered his own share of problems at the Belle Vista Hair Design Academy. His disagreement with some of the school's policies and practices brought him into conflict with several of the administrators, and he did not find it easy to learn basic hairstyling techniques or to get used to the routine on the training floor. But his interest and aptitude for the work kept him going:

> As I went through the program I progressed, but it took some time, you know? I was really slow at first, but that was only because I'm a slow starter. That's just the way I am. I start slow, but once I learn it, I *got* it, you know? Well, the first three months I was on the floor, I had the instructors helping me on every haircut—just about everything I did. But all of a sudden—this really happened within a matter of days—I just broke away. I started doin' things myself and they were turning out real good!
>
> People started noticing me. There were people comin' in askin' for me to work on 'em. I had a clientele that was pretty unusual for someone in that school, and I was selling stuff too. By the time I was there about six months, I was selling a hundred dollars worth of products on the average every week. Fourteen months seemed like a long time to stay there, you know? But I didn't mind it too much. Because when I got to cut, I really impressed myself. And that was enough to keep me going.

Most of Todd's dissatisfaction and difficulty with the hair design program stemmed from a change in school ownership and policies which occurred several months after he enrolled. Todd told me that the advice he got from his CETA counselor, Robbie Anderson, helped him to get through difficult times and resolve some of the problems he was having with school administrators:

> If it wasn't for Robbie, I might have never made it through that school. It would get so mad at the school—at some of the people who were running it—that I couldn't see straight. I'd go down to the CETA center and talk to Robbie about what was going on. He'd listen to me and help me see what was really happening—you know, where I was right about things and where I might be wrong?
>
> See, I had chosen Belle Vista to begin with because they were supposed to be the best. I went around to all the cosmetology schools, and I chose that one. Then Superior bought out Belle Vista about two months after I got there. When they took over, they made big promises, you know? They told us, "You're gonna get the most excellent hairstylist training available in the State of Oregon." So we thought, "Great! This is gonna be terrific!"
>
> But as the changeover was going on, a lot of people started to get discouraged. There were certain classes that we never got. They were going to do *this* and going to do *that,* but they never did. When some of us tried to call 'em on it, they told us they weren't

obligated to honor our contracts with Belle Vista. But they *were*.
They had told us they would honor those contracts, and they were
supposed to give us certain classes. But their attitude was they don't
have to if they don't want to.

Well, I got mixed up in that. I guess they saw me as a ring leader
or somethin', 'cause one of the owners came down pretty hard on
me. There were other things that bothered me, too, about that
place. They treated us like children. They required a doctor's note
every time you were out sick, and they put people on probation for
almost anything. Also there was the fact that some of their instructors weren't even licensed to be instructors. They were stylists from
the Superior Salon down the street. There were lots of things that
made me mad about that place. Their attitude was pretty crummy
as far as I was concerned.

It helped me a lot to talk to Robbie about it. One of the things he
helped me see was that I couldn't fight 'em on everything. He would
say, "You know, you might be right about all these things—you
probably *are* right. But if you try to fight 'em on everything, you're
gonna burn-out there. You can't change everything; you gotta pick
the issue that's most important to you and concentrate on that. I'll
support you if you can prove your case and all. But if you make an
issue out of *everything,* you're just gonna wind up getting thrown
out, you know?"

Robbie was right about that, I think. The main thing really was
the classes, that they should give us all the classes they promised.
There were a couple CETA students in my class, you know? And
Robbie got Jack Bugati to go down there and talk to one of the
owners. In the end, we got just about all of the classes we were
supposed to get, with the exception of manicuring. They said you
had to pay four hundred dollars extra if you wanted a manicuring
class—which wasn't fair at all. But I didn't care that much about
manicuring anyway, so I didn't try to fight it, you know?

Todd graduated from the Superior Academy with state licenses in
cosmetology and hair design. Despite his dissatisfaction with Superior's
policies, Todd feels that the training he got at the academy was generally
of high quality. But he points out that good training as a hairstylist is no
guarantee of employment:

A lot of people have trouble finding work after they get their
license. You have to be able to sell yourself, and you gotta hustle to
build up a clientele. I don't know if you heard about the percentages and averages in this field? About 40 percent of the
students leave school before they've even graduated. Another 20
percent quit the business within about three months after they get

out of school. Then there's about twenty percent who work, but they never really do much of anything with it. Only about 20 percent ever really make it, really apply themselves and have a career in hair design.

Building a clientele is the main thing, you know? And a lot of that is how you apply yourself. If you don't hustle, if you don't make things happen, if you don't go out and talk to people and turn yourself on to them, if you can't come out and say: "Hey, I cut hair, and I'd like to do yours sometime." If you can't do that kind of thing, you're never gonna get anybody except the walk-in trade, and it'll take you forever to build up a clientele.

Todd is determined that he will be among the few in his class who will be able to establish himself successfully as a hair designer. And he found ways to continue his training and develop more sophisticated skills after leaving the hair design academy:

They teach you how to cut and style in school. But they don't really teach you that much about the hair design *business.* I've been learning a lot more about all that since I got out of school. Three months before I graduated from Superior, I met Paul and Louis, the guys I work for now. I met them through a guy I went to school with. I became a model in a hair show they were doing. And from that day, since the hair show, well, I saw what they *did,* you know? And I said, "This is *it!* This is the kind of stuff I want to do!" So I went with them, even though it's a new shop and all. The pay isn't that good—it's gonna take a while to build a clientele. But I'm learning from two people who graduated from the best hair design school in the world. Both Paul and Louis went to Sassoon's in San Francisco. I may not ever have *that* kind of diploma, but I will have that knowledge. I'll have all the techniques that they know, and *that* is going to better me.

What Does It Take to Succeed?

I've learned the hard way that you gotta have the personality to put up with people. There's always problems that you gotta handle, and you can't always say what you think or do what you want. You gotta stay on top of the situation, even though sometimes you feel like gettin' so mad and screamin'. You gotta hold that back, you know? That's really part of any job. There's just a lot of things you gotta be tolerant with. If you wanna succeed at work, you gotta learn how to handle yourself and other people.   *Carrie Green*

Learning how to handle problems is part of life—particularly working life. It is hard to imagine a job without conflict or crisis, or a work situation that does not require self-control, tolerance, and the ability to communicate under pressure. All of the young people in our group encountered problems in their CETA assignments. What they learned about handling themselves and others in critical situations was an important part of their program experience. Many of them learned their lessons the hard way.

Carrie and the others in our group were no strangers to crisis and adversity. From early childhood their lives were filled with conflict—at home, at school, and in the community—and they did not expect their jobs or program assignments to be problem-free. They had learned to expect crises and conflicts, but they had not necessarily learned how to handle them. Their previous experience in informal groups and institutional settings generally did not encourage a belief in solutions. Their ability to effect changes in their own situations or influence the course of external events had often proved to be limited. Some of them had no faith that the problems they faced could be resolved, so they were not inclined to even try to communicate their point of view or find ways to work things out. In times of crisis or potential conflict, their usual pattern had been to fight or flee; and neither of these responses was likely to bring success.

To succeed in their program assignments, the first and most persistent challenge the young people faced was finding ways to reconcile their personalities and lifestyles with the regimen and requirements of the worksite or classroom. Some of the young people received guidance and support from their counselors or work supervisors in making this adjustment. Peggy Bromfield's supervisor counseled her on her drinking problem, supported her through her family crisis, and helped her to develop perspective on her own behavior in the physical therapy ward. But others who faced similar problems had to work things out on their own.

As a seventeen-year-old single parent with little work experience, Carmeletta DeVries had a hard time juggling her CETA job responsibilities with the demands of her infant son and the requirements set by the welfare office. In the six months that she spent working in the hospital cafeteria, Carmeletta never got a clear picture of her supervisor's expectations. She knew that her frequent tardiness and occasional absence could jeopardize her job, but it never occurred to her to sit down with her supervisor and discuss the problems she was having. She tried to handle the situation by herself. When Carmeletta had a conflict that she could not resolve on her own, she decided to quit her job:

> I would have been fired anyway, you know? So there wasn't much I
> could do *but* quit. There didn't seem to be much point in talkin'
> about it. I had never talked too much to my supervisor anyway. A
> couple of times she said that I did good work but I was tardy too

much. On my time card, there was a place, you know, for remarks, but she never evaluated me. So I didn't really know what she thought, but I thought I was doin' pretty good there. But then, after my baby had been sick and I had to miss work a couple times, she got mad at me for not callin' in. I did call up once, you know, but nobody really told me that you were supposed to call before nine o'clock every day you weren't comin'. She told me I would have to be dismissed if I missed work *one* more time.

About three or four weeks after that, I got this card in the mail sayin' that I had to be at the welfare office on Monday mornin'. I tried to call them up and change it to another time. But my case-worker wasn't there, and the woman at the office said it was about Medicaid and that I had to come in or I might be cut off it. I knew that I couldn't be absent from work one more time. It meant I was gonna lose my job; and I had been hopin' to get hired on per-manent, 'cause the pay is pretty good, workin' for the state. But I couldn't afford to lose the Medicaid right then either. I just couldn't see any way out of it—so I quit my job.

Walking away from problems was a behavior pattern that a number of the teen-agers in our group had developed long before they started their CETA assignments. Jack Thrush spent his childhood in a household where problems were not directly acknowledged, and communication among family members was limited. He had a hard time confronting problems in his own life, and he did not expect understanding or support from adults—particularly those in authority. When Jack ran into trouble at home, at school, and, later, on the job, he would try to get away from his problems by temporarily removing himself from the situation. If the problems grew worse—as they usually did—he would simply stay away and try to work things out for himself someplace else.

Jack saw his CETA job as a fresh start. But it was not long before he found himself in the same old pattern:

I thought the job at the senior citizens' center was pretty good. I was real excited about it at first. It was the most I'd ever been paid, you know, and I was workin' nearly full-time. But then I ran into some problems, and I ended up leaving. I don't know. . . . See, the way it was, I had a problem—I guess you could say it was a *com-munication* problem—with the boss there. She seemed like a really nice person and everything, real smart and thoughtful toward others. But I found it hard to talk to her, it seemed like she had a lot to handle or something, you know? I don't know. To me it seems like she didn't quite know where I was at all, and I didn't know where she was at.

The work that I was doin' right before I left was sanding. I was workin' with the electric sander, you know? I didn't like it much. It was makin' me cough, and I—well, I started feeling it was hazardous to my health. I don't know. I just started getting a real negative attitude about the job. I didn't want to bother anybody there. But I stopped comin' in on time, or comin' in at all, and stuff like that. Nobody said anything to me, you know? But I felt I was in a spot.

After I had stayed away from work a couple weeks, my CETA counselor started callin' me up—asking me would I like a different job. I guess I wanted a different job, but I felt like I was lettin' a whole lot of people down at the senior citizen's center. I started looking around for another job on my own. My CETA counselor called me a few more times, but I didn't call him back or go down there or anything. I felt bad about it, you know? The pressure got to me, but I couldn't seem to do anything about it. I wish now that, before I quit, I'd have *talked* to someone or done *something,* instead of just screwin' up.

Most of the young people in our group did not run away from the problems they encountered in their CETA jobs or program assignments. When conflicts developed on the job, some of the young people assumed that *they* were wrong and their supervisors right, or they decided that even if their problems and complaints were justified there was not much chance of their being able to improve the situation or influence the behavior of their supervisors or coworkers. But while some of the young people chose to ignore problems in their program assignments and stick it out as best they could, others were certain that they were right and were determined to fight it out. The several young people in our group who became embroiled in conflicts with their supervisors or other authority figures, but they found out that confrontation was not likely to resolve issues in their favor.

Carrie Green was assigned to a CETA project that was based in a college in Kalamazoo. The design for this project called for rotating job assignments (so that participants could learn and experiment with a variety of different skills) and individual counseling to help the young people collect career information and make appropriate plans. But the design had never been implemented; most of the project participants were given routine clerical assignments and little counseling was provided by the college staff.

On Carrie's first day at the college, she was introduced to Dr. White, the project director, who impressed her as being a "real intelligent and dignified person." Dr. White was responsible for the design and operation of the CETA project. He was the only person on the college staff with the authority to provide direction, settle disputes, or make final decisions about project functions. But Dr. White was a busy man; he had classes to teach, students to advise, meetings to attend, and a book to write. Responsibility for the daily supervision of eight to ten full-time project participants was delegated to a nineteen-year-old secretary, who had held her own job at the college for less than a year. Carrie was not on the job long before she realized that there were going to be problems:

> When I first came on here, you know, there was a pile of work just backed up in the office. I caught on quick to the xeroxing and filing, and I would try to get things cleared away. But finally I had to say, "Hey, I can't *do* all this. This is just too much for me." So they decided that they needed to divide up the work better. But Susan—the girl who was supervisin' us—she would get so hassled that she couldn't communicate. You never know exactly *what* you were supposed to be doin'. Dr. White would come along and say one thing, then Susan would come along and change it.
>
> Susan is Dr. White's secretary, and I guess she was supposed to come around and check up on us and everything. But her attitude was really bad. She'd act like, "I'm the boss here—so do as I say or you'll lose your job!" But she didn't act like a boss, 'cause she'd go runnin' to Dr. White and complain about everything we did instead of talkin' to us about things. If you even went to the bathroom, she thought you were tryin' to get out of work or something. She was hardly older'n us, but she'd treat you like you were a little kid. It was, I don't know, *degrading*—that's what it was. She didn't really *care* about us, you know? This one girl was pregnant, mind you, and she ordered her to get up on a table and put these boxes away on this shelf that was way up by the ceiling.

Carrie was not the only person who was having problems in this project: Confusion was rampant. Participant job functions and learning objectives were never clearly defined. Training was administered only on a haphazard, task-oriented basis. There were no formal policies governing task assignments or supervision. The young secretary who was given the role of a supervisor was clearly overwhelmed. Her decisions often appeared to be arbitrary and were frequently reversed at the last minute. The participants had little respect for her, and they openly challenged her authority and questioned her judgment. Finally, when it was clear that things were really out of hand, Dr. White called the participants together for a meeting.

He asked the CETA participants to express their views about what was wrong with the project. Carrie believed that Dr. White had no idea of what was really going on. She decided to confront him with her true feelings about the situation. But her candor was not well received, and the confrontation only made things worse:

> He said the meeting was to talk about our attitudes and stuff. He knew there had been some problems, and he said he wanted to hear our views on it. I figgered he needed to know, so I just told him how it really *was* there. But he got upset that I spoke up, you know? He got *real* offended, 'cause I told him how the attitude really was and how I think it should change. He looked at me, and his face got red. He stared at me for a long time, and then he said, "Well, if you don't like your job here, you know what you can do." I couldn't believe it. I said, "You're askin' us what's wrong, and we're supposed to be tellin' you. But when you hear it, you can't handle it."
>
> After that, things just got worse—it was like they were just lookin' for me to make trouble. If I was one minute late, they would make sure it was deducted from my pay. But the others had a hard time too, you know? Terry and Anita quit. Sheryl got in a fight with Susan, and she got fired over it. Betty was suspended for five days 'cause she had watched the fight and didn't do nothin' about it. Practically the only people that stayed there were the ones that had kids or something and just couldn't afford to lose the job. I stuck it out for six months, but finally I just had to quit. I realized that it was just never gonna get any better.

When confrontation with Dr. White failed to achieve positive results, Carrie did not report her difficulties to her CETA counselor at the youth program agency. She figured that whatever she faced in her job was *her* problem; and when she could not stick it out any longer, she left.

Sandy Bonds spent three months trying to resolve her conflicts with an unresponsive crew leader before she finally decided that he was blocking her progress and she had the right to go to the project supervisor and request another crew assignment. The day she received her new crew assignment, Sandy told me:

> I can't believe that it was so easy to settle all this and get on a new crew! I've been upset for three months, but I didn't think there was anything I could do about it. I was just tryin' to hang in there, you know, so I wouldn't lose my job or anything. But today, that whole deal about finish work just really blew up, and I finally had to do somethin' about it.
>
> See, about two months ago, I asked my crew leader if I could try some more in-depth work, making patterns and things. He said sure, fine. They set it up for our crew to get the next cabinet job, and he

said I could do it like a special project. Well, the cabinet job has been goin' on for three weeks now. I keep goin' in there to work on 'em, but all I've gotten to do on 'em was put a couple staple guns to 'em and put a little glue on. He won't let me hardly touch 'em. I didn't get the chance to do any, you know, cuttin' out and puttin' together, or any of the figuring for it. I was really unhappy about that!

I tried talkin' to my crew leader about it, you know? As far as I can understand, it's because he decided that he wanted to cut it out and put it together by himself. That really screwed me around, 'cause I thought that he was gonna teach me how to do it, and he ended up doin' the whole thing by himself. We had a number of little arguments about that. He contradicts himself, and it's confusing 'cause ya can't understand what he's tryin' to convey to you.

Then, this morning I heard him say that he didn't think we were capable of doin' that kind of work, and that's why *he* did it. And I thought, here's an instructor that's paid by the public school tellin' me that I'm incapable to do this work, and that's what I'm here to learn. This isn't some joke to me, you know, or some way to pass the time. It pissed me off, you know? I've been here over eight months now listenin' to all his shit about how dumb women are, and there's nothing that he did to those cabinets that I couldn't have done.

I was real upset, so I went up and talked to the supervisor. He and one of the counselors listened to me, and they said they would take me off his crew. I'd been thinkin' I *had* to stick it out, you know. But I've been doin' this crew three months, and I'm tired of doin' so much screwin' around with him. I'm glad about the new crew. It still pisses me off, though, 'cause I feel that he's held me back.

Some of the young people in our group learned to resolve problems and handle crises and went on to complete their program assignments with a sense of success. Those who were able to compromise and work through their conflicts with supervisors or other authorities emerged from their program experience with new insight on themselves and better tools for handling similar situations in the future. Others learned to ignore irritations and problems that seemed to be built into their program assignments and held on to their jobs until they ended or something better came along. Several of the young people dropped out of the program with regrets over their failure to confront problems or communicate effectively with their supervisors and coworkers.

Though their appraisals of their own performance and the quality of their experiences in the program varied widely, most of the young people left their CETA assignments with the belief that interpersonal skills were the key to success in a work environment. These teen-agers agreed that experience, skills, and education are important factors in getting *hired* for a good job; but they believed that ultimate success in the working world depends more on personal qualities and communication skills than on credentials or formal qualifications. Their comments on this subject are emphatic:

> What do you need to succeed? Just knowledge and personality, really. Mainly, you have to know how to *talk* to people. You don't really *have* to have an education, I don't think. If you know how to relate to people and, you know, *communicate,* then I think you can get over in almost any situation.   *Genetta Burke*

> I'd say you gotta be pretty positive and outgoing to succeed. You have to be able to reach out to other people, make yourself clear, to get what you want. Almost any kind of job you get, you gonna have to work with other people. So you gotta be able to communicate with them—and put up with them too, you know?   *Adam Sledge*

> I think you have to be able to put up with a *lot* of stuff from a lot of different people. That takes tolerance and self-confidence. You have to learn to be a "people" person. I don't care what you do, if you're gonna get *anywhere* with it, you have to like people. You have to get along with other people well. You have to be able to *relate* to other people.   *Todd Clinton*

7. Where Do We Go from Here?

On My Way

> Some people have all the right breaks and they still wind up as failures. You can get all the training or education in the world, but if you don't settle down to one thing and really apply yourself, you'll never be successful. I applied myself in hairstyling school, and now I'm applying myself in my job. I *know* I'm gonna succeed.   *Todd Clinton*

It is too soon to forecast the ultimate career success or failure of any of the young people in our group. But it is clear that some have progressed farther than others in establishing viable working lives. While some of the young people are just beginning to think about the future, Todd Clinton, Sven Latoka, and Jean Ansel have already set career goals and are on the way to achieving them.

As he launches his career in hair design, Todd Clinton is also beginning a new family life. Three months after completing his CETA subsidized training, Todd married Patsy, a young woman he met at the hair design academy. The two plan a joint career. While Patsy completes school, Todd is continuing his work with Paul and Louis. Beginning hairstylists do not make much money. To support himself and his new wife, Todd augments his income from the salon with weekend construction work. But Todd takes a broad view of the future. Hair design is not just a job for him; it is a field that combines career potential with the opportunity for creative fulfillment. During our last interview, Todd told me:

> I feel real positive about the future, even though right now I'm working in a job where the pay is terrible. I'll admit it, it's rotten! But, you know, I'm learning from two people who are really tops in hair design, and I'm doing the kind of stuff I really wanna do. I was lucky to get on with stylists of this quality, you know? But still, it's a new shop, and it'll take a year, maybe a year and a half, to build up the clientele.
>
> I want to have a shop of my own someday. I want to be different—not weird or anything—but I want to be really good and to be different, too—to create hair designs that nobody else does, that nobody else *can* do. Hopefully, I can help to make the hair industry

better. This industry is changing. In the past ten years, it's gone from the guys who were seen as sissies when they started, to a career that lots of men take seriously. It's not a sissy business—it's a very *competitive* business and a very *egotistic* business. Everybody's got an ego in this business. I'm no exception. You have to prove that you're good. That takes time.

You know, I always dreamed of going to New York, Chicago, or Los Angeles—being a big success. But lately—especially since I got married—I've calmed down more. Now I think I'd like to set myself up somewhere on the Oregon coast. I'd like to own my own salon there. I want an A-frame salon, and I want an A-frame house. I want two kids and a happy marriage. And I wanna live where there isn't a lot of pollution; where I can raise my kids the way I want to raise them. Patsy and I have talked a lot about it, and we've agreed to spend about five more years in Portland. We figure it'll take at least that long before we know enough and raise enough money to start our own shop.

I'm ambitious in my career, but I really think that to be happily married and to raise kids is the most important thing. I want to own my own salon, but I don't need to be on top, you know? I just want to live and be happy. I don't expect to make seventy-five thousand dollars a year. But I do want to be noticed, and I want to make it as a hair designer. I want people to say: "Todd Clinton? I know him—he's really good!"

Sven Latoka is planning a career in the construction industry. He likes carpentry work and is confident that he will be able to succeed in this field. After eight months in the CETA renovation project, Sven began to look for work on his own. Two weeks before the project ended, he found a full-time job with a private contractor in Jamaica Plain. Though Sven had basic skills and experience in carpentry before he became a CETA participant, he believes that his project experience gave him the additional skills, track record, and connections he needed to land an entry-level job in construction:

I guess you could say that I always wanted to be a carpenter. But for a while there, it didn't look like I was gonna make it. Getting this job from the CETA program was a good break that came at the right time for me—made me realize, you know, that I *could* get a future goin' with it. I was only here for one month when I got promoted. Jim put me in as supervisor 'cause he knows I do good work. You know, I'm pretty smart with this work, too, figurin' out what to do and gettin' the job done. I learn real quick. Jim gave me a good recommendation for what I did here. Without this experience, I doubt I could have gotten the job.

Sven does not expect to start out at the top. Like Todd, he was willing to begin with a relatively low-paying job that would provide the opportunity to prove his competence and refine his skills. Sven believes that the long-range prospects in carpentry are good, and he expects to work his way up:

> In the job I got, I'll be buildin' houses, and that's a new experience for me. With the experience I've had and the stuff I know, I should be makin' about six bucks an hour. But I'm willing to work for less while I'm showin' 'em I can handle the job. They're only payin' me $4.50 an hour to start, you know, but I expect good raises coming. I don't think I'll have no trouble with *that*, 'cause I plan to work *real* hard. When my boss says to go, you know, I'll be the first one up to grab something and get to work.
>
> I think carpentry is the perfect career for me. I want work that I can enjoy. I like carpentry 'cause you do different things all the time. If you do the same thing, it's in a different place—never the *exact* same thing. I want a job to support a family someday, and I think I can get there with carpentry. There's good money in it, you know, if you can make it. I'll make a career as a carpenter with no problems, 'cause I'm a hard worker. I know that.

Jean Ansel plans to continue her work with the hearing-impaired. During her twelve months as a CETA participant, she made remarkable strides in employability development and career planning. Unlike Sven and Todd, Jean entered the CETA program with no specific vocational plans and relatively little work experience. While in the program she received career counseling, academic instruction, vocational training, and intensive work experience. Jean was ready to take advantage of these opportunities. She left the program with a GED, eight community college credits, and a steady job with Portland public schools. She plans to continue working while she goes to college and prepares for a career as an interpreter, and she is looking for ways to expand her learning opportunities on the job:

> I know I want to work with deaf or handicapped people—probably as an interpreter. I want to be an expert at sign language, and that takes years of experience. I'm getting good experience here, but I work with the really slow kids and their language skills are limited. That's why I want to try and see if I can get into the higher level —work with kids at the high school level—here at the school. I'm teaching signing to some of the teachers and that keeps me on my toes. If I was offered a good job interpreting for deaf adults, I would

take it. But as far I know now, I'm stayin' here to work with the children and teach 'em for a few more years.

As for schooling—I plan to continue in night school at the community college until I finish. Then I'll take more classes at the university. I'd like to get an interpreting license. You really only need it if you are going to interpret for legal purposes, but you can also use it in schools or other kinds of interpreting work. Interpreting is my first choice, but I'm also taking education classes in case I end up in teachin'.

You know, here at the school, I'm only getting paid about $150 more a month than when I was in CETA. All the aides complain because, you know, we're actually in the classroom *teachin'* the children all day and yet we get paid less than half what the certified teachers make. The teachers don't do as much classroom work as we do, and they don't make up the program either. We've got other people who do nothing but write the program out on paper. Still the work here—it really has been great for me. I'll keep a lookout for better opportunities, but I'm in no big hurry to leave.

Todd, Sven, and Jean have chosen career roles that are very different, and the routes that they have taken to prepare themselves for these roles also differ. But all three have based their choices on apparently realistic appraisals of their values, needs, and abilities, as well as on a basic understanding of the employment requirements, opportunities, and rewards in their chosen fields. Their participation in CETA program activities represents neither the first nor the last step in the process of developing their skills and establishing their careers. They came into the program with different needs and expectations. But all three emerged with the experience, skills, or credentials they needed to get off the ground and the self-confidence, motivation, and discipline they will need to keep going.

Discovering a Way to Go

The others in our group were not as far along when they left the CETA program. Relatively few teen-agers enter employment and training programs with as much work experience as Sven, or vocational objectives that are as well-defined as Todd's, and most are not able to progress as rapidly and surely in their career development as Jean. But a number of the other young people in our group were able to make significant strides in their efforts to establish a working life. Douglas Giscard, Tien Van Chin, Sandy Bonds, and Felisa Santana all left their program assignments with the qualifications for entry-level employment of some kind, and each is now making tentative career plans.

Douglas is a full-time employee at the Street Shelter in Portland. He enjoys his job and has recently signed up for a community college course on the juvenile justice system. Though the precarious funding situation at the Street Shelter makes his future at the agency far from secure, Douglas says he is not worried. He figures with the knowledge and experience he has gained there, he will be able to find another social service job if he needs one. Douglas once wanted to be a master jewel-thief or a rock star, and he says that he still plans to make a million dollars. But his current goal is to create and administer a model social service agency. During our last interview, Douglas told me:

> I'd like to work my tail off and keep moving up in this field. With the ideas I have, I think I could make the perfect social service agency, or as close to it as possible. Make it unique—set aside from all the others—that's what I'd like to do. I don't know enough to do it now, but I'm learning. I feel confident that I will succeed. There will probably be people standing in my way—there always are, you know? You just have to step over them. I plan to get four years of college, maybe even more—that's anywhere within the next five to ten years. When I get the schooling I need, I can go ahead. If I can get the right grants for it—show the right people that this can really work, convince them that my ideas will work better than any of the other agencies that are around—then they won't be able to refuse me. They'll practically *have* to give me the financial backing and support that I need.

Douglas still has a lot to learn about the realities of social service program-funding and administration. His career scenario will undoubtedly go through changes. But, meanwhile, he has a job he likes, enough income to support himself, and the time to complete his education and consider career possibilities.

Tien Van Chin also has ambitious career plans., He would like some-day to be a United States diplomat. Tien is confident that he will be able to find work as a computer programmer, and he is prepared to work his way through four years or more of schooling at a university. Though he believes that he has the ability to succeed in the international relations field, Tien concedes that many barriers stand in his way. He says:

> A career in international relations is my goal in life—to get the chance to see many different places, meet different kinds of people, learn many languages, see lots of different styles of life. But I'm not sure I can make it; there would be many problems. First, you know, is trouble concerned with race here in United States. They say all people have equal opportunity, but, no, that is not reality. I never

see top people in government departments, like Department of
State, who are Chinese—no, never see Chinese people there. I
believe the country takes, what they call, "natural citizens" first.
This is custom from a long time ago. Condition is getting better,
you know? You may get work in important field, but you might not
get as high because you are not a natural American. Also, actions
and speaking style you must learn if you are not born American.
English is a complicated language.

I really don't know if I can make it or not right now. I have
started actions to become American citizen. I am lucky to have a
skill. When I finish here, I will get work as computer operator and
programmer. Then I will start going to the university at night.
Finishing school I know I can do. About the rest, I will have to see.

Douglas and Tien have high aspirations. Both young men say they
are willing to defer marriage and family life and work their way through
advanced schooling in order to achieve the credentials and qualifications
that they hope will eventually bring them prosperous and satisfying careers.
Sandy Bonds, on the other hand, has no intention of continuing her formal
education; and she has her own definition of career success:

I'm not one of those people that has to bring themselves up higher
and higher to feel successful. To me, workin' at something I like
and doin' it on my own, independently, is what makes me
happy—makes me feel successful. I mean, a lot of people think that
you're not really successful until you're president of the United
States or something, you know? But I don't think that's true. It
really depends on the person. Some people have high hopes and all
that shit for their lives and some people don't. If you wanna get real
deep and heavy about it, I think most everybody's had it ground
into their mind that you gotta keep movin' up the ladder to enjoy
life. But I just wanna be happy where I am. I mean, day by
day—work where I'm happy at, live where I'm happy at—and that's
about it. It's hard for me to explain this—you know, if I wanna
move up the scale or something, I will—but I don't feel that I
have to.

Sandy values independence over upward mobility and financial
success. Though she does not see herself as a striver, she does have an
aspiration: to support herself while working as a finish carpenter. She
realizes that she has some distance to go before she can achieve her goal.
Sandy learned a lot about carpentry during her time in the construction
and home repair project. But before she can expect to be a finish carpenter, Sandy feels she must upgrade her skills and get more experience in
cabinetry:

Bein' in this project has given me a lot of knowledge about crafts-
manship and all, but I feel that the average person leavin' the
program would be lacking the skills to go right out and be a carpenter. I mean, you don't have the level of skills that comes from
doin' each thing over and over to where you can do it perfect every
time—without bendin' nails or breakin' boards or anything like that.
You know, you can't just go up to some contractor and say, "Hey,
gimme a job. I know how to do all this stuff, but it still takes me a
real long time, and every once in a while, I haffta pull out half the
nails I put in."

I'll be leavin' here soon, you know, so I've been tryin' to figger
out what I'm gonna do. Well, I've been talkin' to this cabinetmaker
who has a little shop down the road from here, and he said he
would take me on as assistant for half a year or so—you know, let
me work with him and show me the ropes and stuff. It would be
like an OJT—the CETA program'll pay part of the wages, you
know?

I think it'll work out pretty good. 'Cause I like workin', and I'd
really like to be a finish carpenter, you know, makin' tables, desks,
and cabinets. I don't expect to make much while I'm workin' up my
skills. I'll probably never make much money. But that's no big deal
to me. I'm forced into the whole thing about havin' to make money
to live—everybody is. But I'm not gonna knock myself out to get
rich or anything.

Felisa Santana is different from Sandy. She is filling an occupational
role traditionally reserved for women, and she plans to have a traditional
family life. But her feelings about working are in many ways similar to
Sandy's:

I really like to work, and I enjoy the office work I'm doing. I would
like to do well in my career, but mainly I want to be happy. You
know, I don't really care if I make a lot of money, so long as I'm
happy with the work. I would like, you know, to get married and
have kids. I want us to live in a nice place and to have enough
money. The man that I marry will have a good job, you know? But
I will probably still keep working anyway, 'cause I like to have a
job, and, in most families, I think you really need to have both
people workin'.

Felisa earns $135 a week in her job as a billing clerk. She is still living
at home and has been able to save money. Lately, Felisa says she has begun
to think more about the future. She plans to keep her job at the clinic for
several more years. But she is also considering taking college classes part-
time and hopes to use her clerical skills and experience as a base for
further opportunities.

I like working at the clinic, but sooner or later I will need a change, you know? You can get work in a lot of different places if you know how to do clerical work. I'd like to work some place where you see a lot of different people every day—dealing with the public, you know, not in a clinic but somewhere else. One of the things I've thought about is the airlines. You know how they have billing clerks to take reservations and stuff out at the airport? I think that would be an exciting job. I'd like to find out more about that.

Still Looking

Todd, Sven, and Jean have career plans and are on the way to achieving their goals. Douglas, Tien, Sandy, and Felisa have jobs and are discovering and pursuing career possibilities on their own. What about the others in our group? Some of the young people were not ready or able to make their way in the world of work. Where did they go when they left their CETA assignments? Carmeletta, Carrie, and Adam went out to look for work. Genetta and Peggy continued receiving welfare while they waited to get into other training programs or vocational education classes. Luanne and Bobby both went back to high school. Jack and Harold enlisted in the army. These teen-agers have not given up their hopes for useful working lives, but few of them have definite ideas about what they want or what is possible for them. Most are still looking for a way to go.

Luanne Clawson has not yet settled on career plans, but she is optimistic about the future. At seventeen, she is still living at home and feels that she has plenty of time to finish school and consider various career possibilities. Luanne thinks her nine months in the CETA education and employment project was a good experience, but she has decided to go back to West Roxbury High. During our last interview, Luanne told me:

> I'm goin' on back to school, you know, for my senior year. I think I learned more from the teacher here at the community center than what I was gettin' over at West Roxbury. But I still decided to go back, 'cause graduation's comin' up and all and I want to be with my friends and everything. 'Course, the best thing about it here is my job. I really enjoy workin' in the office. But Mrs. Jackson, she say they can keep me on—maybe workin' for a couple afternoons each week—even if I don't go to school here.
>
> I'm not sure about what I wanna do after I graduate and every-thing. I still plan to keep on workin', you know, but I'm not sure what *as*. I like secretary work pretty good—you know, I wouldn't mind doin' that. But, lately, me and this friend of mine, Frances, we been thinkin' 'bout bein' airline stewardesses—you know, flight attendants? I think that would be a lot of fun.

Genetta Burke is only two years older than Luanne. But her circumstances are different, and she is beginning to feel a sense of urgency about the future:

> I'd like to have my own house, my own yard for my kids to play in, where they'd be safe and off the streets. I'd like to have more money and be able to take my kids more places—stuff like that, you know? I worry about am I gonna be able to make somethin' for myself and my kids? Are we gonna be able to have things? I really wanna get out of Boston. That's my main concern: gettin' out of Boston and takin' up some kinda trade—to know somethin', to be able to move on.

During the nine months that Genetta worked on the weatherization project, she was able to successfully coordinate childcare and other family responsibilities with the demands of a daily work regimen. She completed a GED, and she felt good about earning a weekly paycheck. But when the weatherization project ended, Genetta's employment future was still uncertain. Genetta feels that she needs more training to qualify for the kind of job that would allow her to move off the welfare rolls. Her weatherization crew supervisor, Henry, has promised to help her get into some kind of training or vocational education program. But Genetta is having a hard time settling on a vocational choice. At this point, she knows more about what she doesn't want than about what she would like to do:

> Well, I found out that I don't wanna do weatherization work! I wanna get into another trainin' program, you know? Henry said they would help me get into some kind of school for whatever kind of trainin' I wanted to do after the project ended. I'm still thinkin' about that. I've worked, you know, here and other places, but I haven't really done things that I want to do. I don't really know all there is to do, and I don't remember seein' anything particular that I'm really interested in.
>   Henry wants me to go to executive typin' school. He thinks I should be an executive secretary, you know? When I was still in high school, I wanted to be a secretary; and I took up typin' for two years. But now I changed my mind. I don't know now, I don't think I have the patience for it. I don't think I'd like somebody dictatin' to me. Sittin' in an office all day—I'd go crazy. Henry always says I think that *I* should be the boss. I have problems with my attitude, you know? I'd rather be workin' with kids than most adults—little kids—maybe babies or retarded kids. I think maybe I'd be pretty good at that.

Peggy Bromfield is also worried about her future. Like Genetta, she has the needs of her two children to consider. Peggy left the medical careers project in Portland with a good idea of what she wanted to do, but she hasn't been able to put it together for herself:

I was pretty excited about bein' a physical therapist assistant. I didn't want to leave my CETA job at the hospital, but the project was ending—you know, it was only supposed to be a temporary thing. Just before the end, you were supposed to go out and find out about a job or further training on your own. I went up to the community college to find out more about their physical therapist program, you know, whether I could get in and could get any money to go to school there. I even talked to my welfare worker about it. And I went around to some of the chiropractors and private clinics to see if there was any jobs available.

Like I said, I was pretty excited about it. But then I started to get discouraged. I realized that it would take me at least two years, goin' to school full-time, to get an assistant's license, and I found out in June that there was no way I could get the money to start until October. I also found out that I can't get any money for babysittin' while I'm in school, so I don't know what I would do with the kids, you know?

I was thinkin' about gettin' part-time work—like in a clinic or something—while I went to school. Most of the places I talked to had a regular therapist. The rest—the smaller places like chiropractors and stuff—worked with part-time people sometimes, but they wanted a license plus several years' experience. The worst thing I found out was that in most places—even with a license —they only pay about five dollars an hour, and a lot of licensed people only work part-time.

It just doesn't sound very good at this point. I think probably the best thing would be for me to go ahead and go for a regular therapist license. But that takes four years, and I just don't see how I could do it now. I doubt they would let me stay on welfare while I went to college for four years, you know? Anyway, I wanna get off welfare. Last week, this friend of mine told me about a factory job that pays $6.50 an hour. Her brother-in-law is a manager there, and she said that he could probably get me on. I'm gonna talk to him. And if it works out, I think I'll go ahead and take it.

The high-paying factory job fell through, and Peggy remained on welfare and out of school. Her efforts to make work-related decisions and get career plans off the ground were further confused by her desire to establish a relationship that would fulfill her needs for companionship and emotional support. The last time we talked, Peggy told me:

I've decided to move down to Roseburg with Ted. He moved in with me, you know, about three months after I finished my job at the hospital. But he's been down in Roseburg for a few weeks now, and he wants me to come there and live. You know, he's been really good to the kids and I feel that he really loves me. He's not crazy about the idea of me workin', you know? He says if I go down there with him, I can get off welfare and he'll support us. I know it's a big risk in a way for me to pick up and go down there. But he has a good job there and everything. I really care about him, you know, and I don't wanna take the chance of losing him.

Some of the young men in our group who were having difficulty settling on career objectives viewed the military service as an alternative to unemployment or low-paying jobs in the secondary labor market. Harold Thomas had no definite career plans. His most successful work experience had been in the army reserves. Upon returning to Boston after his initial stint in the army he enrolled in the Victoria Point weatherization project with limited objectives: to support himself while studying for a GED certificate that would enable him to enter the regular army on favorable terms. He spent five months in the project and, while he does not think much of the work experience he got there, he *was* able to achieve his immediate objectives. Harold is eager to leave Boston and get back to military life. He hopes that his experience in the army will help him decide on a career:

I think the army is where I can find myself. That's why I can hardly wait to get back—to find myself—find out what I really wanna do. I know I'm real good at music and art—nobody can take that away from me, you know? But I don't expect to make a livin' that way or nothin'. I'll be in the army four years this time. If I like it, I'll just reenlist for another hitch. Then if I decide I've had enough, I'll just go to college, and they'll pay part of my educational fees. From there, I really don't know. Maybe I'll be about ready to die. [laughter] I'll be too old for anything else!

Harold has reason to believe that military life will suit him. But the army seems a strange choice for somebody like Jack Thrush. Jack left school because he disliked the regimentation and authoritarian structure, and he had a hard time taking direction, communicating, and fitting into the routine of a steady job. After he walked off his janitorial job at the senior citizens' center in Kalamazoo, he was unable to find work. Jack knows that he has problems, and he feels that so far in his life he has failed to make the best use of his opportunities. He seems to see the army as both a last resort and an opportunity to prove himself. If he can make it in the army, Jack hopes it will give him a start on a better life:

> I been thinkin' about it a long time. I'm real tired of screwin' up all the time, you know? I know a lot of people who've been in the army and it seems to get them straightened out some. My CETA counselor talked to me about it once, and that made me think more about it. I called the recruiter a couple times, you know, and talked to him about it. Then last week, I just went down there. I wanted to look into it really heavy, and I did and decided that I wanted to go ahead and join up.
>
> I've worried about, you know, am I gonna be able to handle it— from not having had that much discipline before and all. But I think maybe I might be able to accept it, because I've never accepted it before. It might be somethin' new for me. I don't know, but I'm gonna give it my best shot, you know? It's the last thing I can think of, and I really want it. I don't wanna screw up at all. I've thought about the bad things that could happen—suppose I ended up in Fort Leavenworth or got a bad discharge or somethin'? But I've been tryin' to think more or less positive.
>
> When I get out of the army, I don't know *what* I'll do. I hope I'm in a better position than I am now. I'd like to have my own house someday, and a really nice job, and maybe a family, too. I think I'd like an outdoor job, and I don't wanna live anywhere near Kalamazoo or any other city. But I feel like the future's gonna be kinda unsteady for me, and I'm not sure what's gonna happen, you know? I hope things are better when I get out of the army.

Carrie Green's hopes for the future are similar to Jack's. She is still looking for a steady job that will provide her the income to support herself and the opportunity to work her way up. She quit her job on a problem-ridden CETA project after only six months. When we met for our last interview, Carrie said she had been looking for work on her own for more than ten weeks. Now that she is eighteen, Carrie feels she has a chance for better-paying factory work. But one prospective job fell through when Susan, her former supervisor at the college, gave her a poor employment reference. This is what Carrie says about her employment plans:

> I have a chance to get into the Clark Company, 'cause my dad knows the production manager there. They pay five dollars eighty-five cents an hour. But I wouldn't really want to work the machines there. You gotta know what you're doin' on the machines—my cousin got a piece of metal right through his hand doin' that. What I'd be doin' is—well, you know how the stock comes out of the machine—whatever it is? Well, I'd bag it and pack it—or

maybe feed the machine the material. That wouldn't be too bad.

What I'd really like is to find a job that I could be happy with—you know, *satisfied* with for a while. 'Cause most jobs that I've had, I *haven't* really been happy with, like at the college. I don't know why, but they treated you lower than everyone else 'cause you were on CETA. If I could have got hired there and I wasn't in a special program, maybe it would have been different, you know?

From the clerical job I had there, I learned that it takes a lot of training to be really good at secretarial work. If I wanted to work in an office, I'd have to get my GED and then go on to college and take typing, bookkeeping, and shorthand. In an office, you're sittin' down all the time. But in a factory, you're standin' up and workin' with your hands. And the money's better in a factory, you know?

That's real important to me 'cause I'd like to get lots of things. My sister, you know, she's almost twenty-five and still livin' at home. By that time, I wanna have a house—even if I have to struggle to work for it. So maybe it has to be a factory job—which I don't really *want* to do, but I'll resort to for a while 'cause it's really good money. It'll get me by, you know?

Carmeletta DeVries also went out looking for work in Kalamazoo after she lost her CETA job at the hospital. She did not have much luck. Carmeletta has less work experience than Carrie. She knows how much she wants to earn and what she wants to do with the money, but she has no career plans and little knowledge about what kind of work is available. Carmeletta knows she would be better off with more education and training, but she is impatient to be out working and earning a paycheck:

I'd like to move out of my sister's house—you know, try to get an apartment and just get pretty much straightened around. I wanna try to get my driver's license and get me some kind of small car that'll get me around and everything. I'd like to get a job that pays five or six dollars an hour, 'cause I don't wanna be on AFDC anymore—I don't like it. I wanna try to be out on my own, you know?

I would do any kind of work, really. All they have to do is teach me, if that's what it takes. It wouldn't make no difference to me, really—long as I knew what I was supposed to be doin'. I used to type some, so I've thought about secretarial work, you know? I can type pretty good—if I look at the keys. You know, I have to read the whole sentence and then type it out? I know I should get more education first. I do plan to get my GED sometime. But right now, I just wanna get me a job.

Jack, Carrie, and Carmeletta's aspirations seem modest in comparison
with those of Adam Sledge. As the completion date for the Victoria Point
weatherization project approached, Adam felt pretty successful. He was
the most competent worker on his crew. He had also managed to earn his
GED certificate and hold down an additional part-time job as a security
guard in the project. Adam is ambitious—he expects to make a lot of
money. He has confidence in his ability to succeed, but he does not have
much knowledge of the working world on which to base his expectations.
Adam told me:

> You know, I done so good here that I been thinkin' maybe I'd get
> into MIT or some other college and take up a degree in weateriza-
> tion. I'd really like to go to school, you know, but I'm more in-
> nerested in makin' some good money. I wanna make ten dollars or
> somethin' an hour to start and then go up higher. Stayin' alive is the
> main thing, you know? The dollar—this day 'n time, that's what the
> world is built on. Everybody wants the dollar, and I'm no different.
> I wanna be livin' it up when I'm older—just doin' what I want,
> whatever I felt in my mind to do—ownin' me a nice car, diamonds,
> jewels. 'Cause I *know* I'll have the money by then—I'll be more
> experienced and everything. Ain't nothin' gonna hold me back.

Bobby Jones's expectations are even greater than Adam's. Since he
was a small boy, Bobby has had one ambition: to become well-known and
financially successful as a professional athlete. The scenario goes like this:
While playing high school ball, Bobby will be spotted by a college scout.
He will be awarded a scholarship and become a college basketball star.
After three or four years, he'll be picked up by a professional club, who will
offer him a fat contract and the chance to step into the bright lights of
fame.

During his two years on the streets as a ninth-grade dropout, and his
year of remedial education and half-hearted work experience as a CETA
participant, Bobby's expectations did not change. When he left the CETA
project, Bobby was reading and writing at about the fifth- or sixth-grade
level. School administrators at West Roxbury High agreed to reenroll him
on a provisional basis as a twelfth-grade student. Bobby was nineteen
years old, and—as far as he was concerned—the scenario was about to
unfold:

> I just wanna be *known*—on the court and off the court—be myself,
> have everyone likin' me—that's about it. 'Course money is real
> important, too, 'cause anything I want to do has to have money.
> Once I make my name, I'd like to build a school named after me. I
> want a big house and lots of things. And I'd like to give things to

people who don't have 'em, you know? I'd like to work in poor
areas, especially here in Massachusetts.

I don't think it's no way I couldn't make it—I don't. I guess I'd
have to think about that if it happen, but right now I just don't
believe it could go wrong. See, next year in high school, I'll play
basketball and football—do real well, have my skills brung
out—and everything'll work out just fine. Once I get to college, I
know things will be hard. But, you know, with help from the
teachers and stuff like that, I'll make it okay. I won't have no
problems playin' basketball. See, the better the people are that I'm
with, the better I play. Once somebody show me somethin' then it's
easy for me to do. It wouldn't be nothin' like that to stop me, you
know? I'll always have the tools. Any good coach could see it—any
good coach.

A Final Note about Programs

In the best of all possible worlds, there would probably be no targeted
youth employment and training programs. If all children grew up in families
that were stable, supportive, and economically secure, lived in communities
that viewed young people as valuable resources, attended schools that
were able to challenge their minds and engage their interests in learning,
and eventually entered labor markets that provided ample entry-level jobs
and opportunities for advancement without regard to age, race, or national
origin, then there would be no need for programs like CETA. In an actual
and imperfect world, these programs represent an attempt to mitigate the
effects of complex and long-standing problems.

No program can redress all the inequities of life in our society. Six
months, twelve months, or even two years in a program will not wipe out
the disadvantages that come from a childhood and adolescence of poverty,
discrimination, or neglect. Youth employment and training programs do
not work miracles, but the services they provide can make critical differences in the lives and employment futures of young people seeking ways
to enter the mainstream of society. For teen-agers like Felisa, Sandy, Jean,
and Douglas, CETA programs provided a pathway to the world of classrooms, worksites, and career possibilities when other routes were blocked
and other institutions had failed.

To say that any program is better than none would be overstating the
case. In a climate where resources for human development are scarce,
inefficiency, incompetency, and insensitivity cannot be defended and should
not be excused. Shortcomings in program conception, design, and execu-
tion are not difficult to find. Some of the ways in which youth employment
programs falter or fail are documented by the stories in this book. For

young people such as Jack, Carrie, Genetta, Carmeletta, and Bobby, CETA participation was a less-than-successful venture. But, despite the short-comings of their program experience, it is still possible to see ways in which each of them gained something.

Bobby Jones may have emerged from eleven months in a CETA project still looking for the coach who would recognize his potential, develop his athletic skill, and set him on the pathway to superstardom. But he also learned to read and write well enough to make further education or training feasible, and he regulated his life-style and developed enough self-discipline to render the possibility of maintaining a working life more realistic. His involvement in the CETA project got him off the street, interrupted his pattern of idleness and growing involvement in criminal life, and put him back in touch with adults who had some concern for his development and well-being.

That there are ways that employment and training programs could better serve young people like Bobby goes almost without saying. It is no accident that some programs are better than others. Young people at various stages of employability and career readiness enter employment and training programs with different needs and capabilities. The programs that work best are those that provide the most individual service and that offer access to the widest range of employment experiences and training oppor-tunities, while encouraging young people to assume responsibility for their own career development as quickly as possible.

An ideal youth employment and training system would include com-munity or neighborhood centers that would provide efficient access to a comprehensive set of services, rather than piecemeal recruitment for isolated projects with limited service capabilities. Young people entering the system would receive counseling to help them evaluate their previous experience, consider their interests and needs, assess their capabilities, and preview their employment and training options before being assigned to program components or activities. With these insights, and under the guidance of their program counselor, participants would define their own learning objectives and commit themselves to achieving them. Program assignments would reflect needs or interests identified in the assessment process, and they would be changed or upgraded as participants set new goals and made progress in achieving their learning objectives. This does not mean that all employment and training opportunities would be created on an individual basis, or that all needed services would be provided directly by the neighborhood program center. But it does imply the im-portance of localizing access to an array of services, and the coupling or sequentializing of services to meet individual needs.

The neighborhood program center could provide sheltered employment and learning experiences for those who need it; but these activities
should serve as a bridge to outside resources and opportunities, rather than
as an isolation or aging vat. For some young people, project work experience in a neighborhood setting is the most appropriate first step in
employability development. Project participation could be effectively linked
with intensive remedial education on an individual basis or in a supportive
classroom. But the young people would also be encouraged to leave their
neighborhoods to collect information about the world of work and find out
more about career alternatives in their communities. Through participation
in job-finding workshops, structured career-planning, and individual research, the young people would prepare themselves to move into full- or
part-time jobs, participate in vocational training programs, or attend community college classes. The youth program system would be able to facili-
tate connections with prospective employers, schools, and training programs in both the public and private sector. While some young people
would require intensive services and program support over a several-year
period, others would be ready to find interim jobs and begin to define and
achieve career objectives on their own with only short-term counseling and
support from the program system.

There is nothing particularly innovative or controversial in the basic
features of this model youth employment and training system. The ideas
underlying the comprehensive program model have been recognized for
years by youth program planners, administrators, counselors, and evalua-
tors. Many of its features have been adopted by local program sponsors
with varying degrees of effectiveness. It seems clear, however, that youth
employment programs, as practiced across our country—particularly in
our urban centers—fall far short of what is possible, or even acceptable.
And it is apparent that to achieve a nationwide network of effective and
comprehensive youth employment and training systems would require
major revisions in program funding, legislation, administration, and service-
delivery practices. It would also require a strong commitment—at the
national, state, and local levels—to meeting the needs of young people who
are outside the mainstream of our society.

Unfortunately, it does not seem too pessimistic to say that, in this time
of government crisis and eroding support for human service programs,
such a commitment appears unlikely. Program reforms are needed, and, in
the long run, it would make economic, as well as humanitarian, sense to
deal with youth employment needs and problems in a comprehensive
fashion. But short of major breakthroughs in federal, state, or local policy,
there *are* ways that individual program counselors, teachers, employers,

and supervisors can make a difference in the lives and employment futures of young people outside the mainstream.

Those who work directly with youth program participants on a day-to-day basis have the greatest opportunity to affect the young people's outlook on themselves and their understanding of the world. They also bear the brunt of the responsibility to humanize and upgrade program services. In their efforts to respond to individual needs and circumstances and to provide appropriate and effective services, those on the front lines may be limited by the constraints of program funding, regulations, or delivery mechanisms; but they should not be guided by these constraints. They must find ways to broaden access to resources, adapt service strategies, and make the system work for the young people they are charged with serving. The challenge is not to match young people with specific jobs, training programs, or career choices, but to assist them in preparing for a lifetime of working and making effective career decisions.

Bobby, Sandy, Carmeletta, and the other young people in our group are survivors. If they are blocked in their attempts to enter the mainstream and establish useful working lives, they will find other ways to survive. But it is we who lose if their efforts are thwarted, their energies misdirected, and their potential wasted on the margins of society.

Bibliographical Essay

While *Hard Knocks* is based primarily upon interviews and firsthand observations of young people, the consultation of works by others has also played an important role in the preparation of this book. In providing a bibliography, my intention is both to acknowledge those authors and works that were of value to me and to provide a resource listing for the reader who desires a better understanding of the employment problems of young people outside the mainstream and the program tools that have been developed and tested for meeting the needs of this group.

The body of literature on adolescent development and the influence of family background, schooling, and community environment on the personal and professional lives of young adults is vast. It is augmented by a substantial, though more recently initiated, archive of research on youth employment problems and programs. The bibliography that follows is selective rather than exhaustive. Though a number of works from the 1960s are listed—including the pivotal studies of James Coleman, Christopher Jencks, and others on equality of educational opportunity, I have concentrated primarily on works completed since the mid-1970s, when youth unemployment reached epidemic proportions, our awareness of the problems faced by low-income teen-agers, minorities, and high-school dropouts expanded, and pressures for a national youth policy increased.

The bibliography is divided into major subject areas. The first area includes works on family experience and adolescent development. Works that I found particularly helpful in this area include Kenneth Keniston's Carnegie Council report on the American family and articles from *Family Planning Perspectives* (1978, 10), by Card, Wise, Furstenberg, Crawford, Moore, and others, on the impact of adolescent parenthood. Levitan and Belous (1981) provide a useful, updated analysis of trends in American family life.

The second area in the bibliography addresses issues of youth in the community. Edward Wynne (1978) writes vividly of the effects of youth alienation. Mangum and Seniger (1978) document the limited opportunities for black urban youth and the problems of life in the ghetto. In separate studies, Barton (1976) and Greenberg (1978) describe how the scarcity of jobs for youth, accompanied by the deterioration of ties to family or school, influence juvenile delinquency. Kohler and Dollar (1978) provide evidence that youth service work can be an antidote to alienation.

In the area of education, Charles Silberman's *Crisis in the Classroom* (1970) stands out as a classic among the many works that attempt to analyze the failings of the public school system and set new directions for education. In a 1971 report on the *Youth in Transition* study, conducted by the Institute for Social Research, University of Michigan; Bachman, Green, and Wirtanen provide an excellent exploratory analysis of the causes and consequences of high school noncompletion (*Dropping Out: Problem or Symptom?*). In more recent works, Barton and Fraser (1980), Kerr (1977), Lasch (1978), and others explore the relationship between secondary schooling and the world of work. Sidney Marland (1974) recommends career education as a program for reforming the public school curriculum, and Ronald Bucknam (1978) suggests the widespread adoption of an experience-based career education model. In a Carnegie Council report (1979), Grasso and Shea assess the impact of vocational education and training on youth. A report on the secondary school guidance system in California prepared by the Open Road organization (1979) is critical of the quality of services provided to minority, low-income, and non-college-bound students. Levine and Havighurst (1977) consider the impact of desegregation efforts on big-city schools and suggest alternative approaches to integration. Schneider (1978) reports on programs to reduce dropout rates and prepare students for adulthood that have been successfully implemented in the Portland public schools.

The advent of the Youth Employment and Demonstration Projects Act of 1977 (YEDPA) triggered an explosion in the volume of research on youth employment and training. From 1978 through 1980 the U.S. Department of Labor, primarily through its Office of Youth Programs, commissioned scores of youth-needs assessments, policy studies, program evaluations, and guidebooks on program development and implementation. The results of much of this work, in final or interim form, were published by the Employment and Training Administration, USDOL in a series of Youth Knowledge Development reports. These reports were distributed by the Office of Youth Programs during the latter part of 1980 and early 1981 and can be obtained currently through the U.S. Government Printing Office.

The Youth Knowledge Development series includes a number of excellent reports and constitutes a remarkable addition to the literature on youth employment; however, the impact of this collection to date has been relatively slight. This is true for a number of reasons: The sheer volume of material is intimidating to the potential user, and the lack of a descriptive index or guide makes it difficult to assess the quality or utility of individual reports. Moreover, the reports were distributed to program agencies and research organizations in the employment and training fields at a time when funding was being cut back and future initiatives were in jeopardy. The current preoccupation with survival has served to sharply curtail efforts to digest information and to expand the understanding of youth employment issues.

I found the following Youth Knowledge Development reports to be rich sources of information on youth employment and unemployment problems: *The Youth Employment Problem: Dimensions, Causes, and Consequences,* prepared by the National Bureau of Economic Research (1980), and *Youth Employment: Its Measurement and Meaning,* prepared by the U.S. Office of Youth Programs (1980). In a 1976 paper, Parnes and Kohen provide a longitudinal analysis of the labor market experiences of noncollege youth, and more recent data from national longitudinal surveys are presented in Youth Knowledge Development reports written by Endriss and Froomkin (1980) and the Center for Human Resource Research, Ohio State University (1980). Three reports from the Youth Knowledge Development series—*Factbook on Youth,* prepared by the Office of Assistant Secretary for Policy, Evaluation and Research, USDOL (1980); *Schooling and Work among Youth from Low-Income Households,* written by Suzanne Barclay and others (1980); and Westat's report on the characteristics of youth enrolled in CETA programs (1980)—provide statistical data that are helpful in assessing special target group needs.

In the area of federal policy studies and program recommendations, several works stand out. The report and recommendations of the Carnegie Council on Policy Studies in Higher Education (1979) is a comprehensive analysis of the needs of young Americans and the options for federal education, work, and service policies. The National Child Labor Committee and National Urban League (1978) and the Potomac Institute's Committee for the Study of National Service (1979) advocate the establishment of a comprehensive national policy in regard to the development, education, and employment of youth. Robert Taggart's *Youth Knowledge Development Report 2.12* (1980) outlines desirable directions for youth employment policies and programs in the 1980s.

At the present time it is difficult to predict the direction of youth employment policies in the 1980s. It appears likely, however, that any initiatives in the near future will call for greater participation from the private sector. Insights regarding the means and potential effects of expanding private sector involvement are provided by the National Commission for Manpower Policy's *An Enlarged Role for the Private Sector in Federal Employment and Training Programs* (1978). In volume 2.16 of the Youth Knowledge Development series (1980), Butler and Darr report on the perspectives of educators and private employers in regard to youth employment issues. Readers who are interested in following congressional efforts to design and enact new youth employment legislation are advised to consult current issues of the *Employment and Training Reporter* and the *Manpower and Vocational Education Weekly.*

The bibliography also includes listings of recent works that may be helpful to professionals involved in program design, development, and delivery as well as program reviews and evaluations that may be of interest to researchers, program planners and operators. Finally, I have included in the bibliography a short list of works on research and program evaluation techniques. The works of Bogdan and Taylor (1975), Douglas (1970), Filstead (1980), and Lofland (1971) on qualitative methods were extremely helpful to me in designing and conducting the research for this book.

Bibliography

Family Experience/Adolescent Development:

Bachman, Jerald G.; O'Malley, Patrick M.; and Johnston, Jerome. *Youth in Transition.* Vol. 6: *Adolescence to Adulthood: Change and Stability in the Lives of Young Men.* Ann Arbor: Institute for Social Research, University of Michigan, 1978.

Card, Josephina J., and Wise, Lauress L. "Teenage Mothers and Teenage Fathers: The Impact of Early Childbearing on the Parent's Personal and Professional Lives." *Family Planning Perspectives* 10 (1978): 199-205.

Fraiberg, Selma. *Every Child's Birthright: In Defense of Mothering.* New York: Basic Books, 1977.

Friedenberg, Edgar Z. *Coming of Age in America: Growth and Acquiescence.* New York: Random House, 1963.

Furstenberg, Frank F., Jr., and Crawford, Albert G. "Family Support: Helping Teenage Mothers to Cope." *Family Planning Perspectives* 10 (1978): 322-33.

Ginott, Haim G. *Between Parent and Teenager.* New York: Macmillan Co., 1969.

Hoffman, Lois Wladis, and Nye, F. Ivan. *Working Mothers: An Evaluative Review of the Consequences for Wife, Husband, and Child.* San Francisco: Jossey-Bass, 1974.

Jencks, Christopher. *Inequality: A Reassessment of the Effect of Family and Schooling in America.* New York: Basic Books, 1972.

Keniston, Kenneth, and the Carnegie Council on Children. *All Our Children: The American Family under Pressure.* New York: Harcourt Brace Jovanovich, 1977.

Levitan, Sar A., and Belous, Richard S. *What's Happening to the American Family?* Baltimore: The Johns Hopkins University Press, 1981.

Moore, Kristin A. "Teenage Childbirth and Welfare Dependency." *Family Planning Perspectives* 10 (1978): 233-35.

Rains, Prudence Mors. *Becoming an Unwed Mother.* Chicago: Aldine Publishing Co., 1971.

Zelnick, Melvin, and Kantner, John Frederick. "Contraceptive Patterns and Premarital Pregnancy among Women Aged 15-19 in 1976." *Family Planning Perspectives* 10 (1978): 135-42.

Youth in the Community:

Barton, Paul E. *Juvenile Delinquency, Work, and Education.* Unpublished report prepared for the U.S. Department of Health, Education, and Welfare. Washington, D.C.: National Manpower Institute, 1976.

Bullock, Paul. *Aspirations vs. Opportunity: "Careers" in the Inner City.* Ann Arbor: Institute of Labor and Industrial Relations, University of Michigan-Wayne State University, 1973.

Cottle, Thomas J. *Children in Jail: Seven Lessons in American Justice.* Boston: Beacon Press, 1977.

Curtis, Lewis. *Violence, Race, and Culture.* Lexington, Mass.: Lexington Books, 1975.

Greenberg, David F. "Delinquency and the Age Structure of Society." In *The Value of Youth,* edited by A. Pearl, D. Grant, and E. Wenk. Davis, Calif: International Dialogue Press, 1978.

Hirschi, Travis. *Causes of Delinquency.* Berkeley and Los Angeles: University of California Press, 1971.

Johnston, Jerome, and Bachman, Jerald G. *Youth in Transition.* Vol. 5: *Young Men and Military Service.* Ann Arbor: Institute for Social Research, University of Michigan, 1972.

Kim, Choong So, and Nestel, Gilbert. *Youth Knowledge Development Report 2.8: The All-Volunteer Force: A 1979 Profile and Some Issues.* Prepared for the Center for Human Resource Research, under contract to the U.S. Department of Labor. Washington, D.C.: U.S. Department of Labor, Employment and Training Administration, 1980.

Kohler, Mary Conway, and Dollar, Bruce. "Youth Service Work: An Antidote to Alienation." In *From Youth to Constructive Adult Life: The Role of the Public School,* edited by R. W. Tyler. Berkeley: McCutchan, 1978.

Mangum, Garth L., and Seniger, Stephen F. *Coming of Age in the Ghetto.* Baltimore: The Johns Hopkins University Press, 1978.

O'Gorman, Ned. *The Children Are Dying.* New York: The New American Library, 1978.

Simpson, Jon E., and Van Arsdol, Maurice D., Jr. "Residential History and Educational Status of Delinquents and Nondelinquents." *Social Problems* 15 (1967): 25-40.

Wynne, Edward A. "Beyond the Discipline Problem: Youth Suicide as a Measure of Alienation." In *The Value of Youth,* edited by A. Pearl, D. Grant, E. Wenk. Davis, Calif.: International Dialogue Press, 1978.

Education:

Bachman, Jerald G.; Green, Swayzer; and Wirtanen, Ilona D. *Youth in Transition.* Vol. 3: *Dropping Out: Problem or Symptom?* Ann Arbor: Institute for Social Research, University of Michigan, 1971.

Barton, Paul E., and Fraser, Bryna Shore. *Youth Knowledge Development Report 2.4: Between Two Worlds: Youth Transition from School to Work.* Prepared for the National Manpower Institute. Washington, D.C.: U.S. Department of Labor, Employment and Training Administration, 1980.

Boston Public High Schools: A Guide for Parents and Students. Prepared by the Citywide Educational Coalition. Boston: Boston School Department, 1979.

Bowles, Samuel. "Toward Equality of Educational Opportunity." *Harvard Educational Review* 38 (1968): 89-99.

Bucknam, Ronald. "Experience-Based Career Education." In *The Value of Youth,* edited by A. Pearl, D. Grant, and E. Wenk. Davis, Calif.: International Dialogue Press, 1978.

Children's Defense Fund. Washington Research Project. *Children out of School in America.* Washington, D.C.: The Fund, 1974.

Coleman, James S. *Equality of Educational Opportunity.* 2 vols. Washington, D.C.: U.S. Government Printing Office, 1966.

Conant, James Bryant. *Slums and Suburbs: A Commentary on Schools in Metropolitan Areas.* New York: McGraw-Hill, 1961.

The Education of Adolescents: The Final Report and Recommendations of the National Panel on High School and Adolescent Education. Washington, D.C.: U.S. Office of Education, 1976.

Grasso, John T., and Shea, John R. *Vocational Education and Training: Impact on Youth.* Berkeley: Carnegie Council on Policy Studies in Higher Education, 1979.

Jencks, Christopher, and Brown, M. D. "Effects of High Schools on Their Students." *Harvard Educational Review* 45 (1975): 273-324.

Jennings, Wayne, and Nathan, Joe. "Some Disturbing Research on School Program Effectiveness." *The Value of Youth,* edited by A. Pearl, D. Grant, and E. Wenk. Davis, Calif.: International Dialogue Press, 1978.

Kerr, Clark. "Education and the World of Work: An Analytical Sketch." In *Access, Systems, Youth, and Employment,* edited by J. A. Perkins and B. B. Burn. International Council for Educational Development, 1977.

Knowles, Asa S., and Associates. *Handbook of Cooperative Education.* San Francisco: Jossey-Bass, 1971.

Lasch, Christopher. *The Culture of Narcissism: American Life in an Age of Diminishing Expectations.* New York: W. W. Norton, 1978.

Levine, D. U., and Havighurst, R. J. *The Future of Big-City Schools: Desegregation Policies and Magnet Alternatives.* Berkeley: McCutchan, 1977.

Marland, Sidney Percy, Jr. *Career Education: A Proposal for Reform.* New York: McGraw-Hill, 1974.

Open Road. *Lost in the Shuffle: A Report on the Guidance Systems in California Secondary Schools.* Santa Barbara: Citizen's Policy Center, 1979.

Peshkin, Alan. *Growing Up American: Schooling and the Survival of Community.* Chicago: University of Chicago Press, 1978.

Reubens, Beatrice G. "Vocational Education for *All* in High School?" In *Work and the Quality of Life: Resource Papers for Work in America,* edited by J. O'Toole. Cambridge, Mass.: MIT Press, 1974.

Schneider, Eugene. "Programs for Transition to Adulthood in the Portland Public Schools." In *From Youth to Constructive Adult Life: The Role of the Public School,* edited by R. W. Tyler. Berkeley: McCutchan, 1978.

Silberman, Charles E. *Crisis in the Classroom: The Remaking of American Education.* New York: Random House, 1970.

Youth Employment/Unemployment Problems:

Adams, Arvil V., and Mangum, Garth L. *The Lingering Crisis of Youth Unemployment.* Kalamazoo, Mich.: The W. E. Upjohn Institute of Employment Research, 1978.

Becker, Brian E., and Hills, Stephen M. "Today's Teenaged Unemployed—Tomorrow's Working Poor?" *Monthly Labor Review,* January 1979, pp. 69-71.

Center for Human Resource Research, Ohio State University. *Youth Knowledge Development Report 2.7; Findings of the National Longitudinal Survey of Young Americans, 1979.* Washington, D.C.: U.S. Department of Labor, Employment and Training Administration, 1980.

Endriss, J. R., and Froomkin, Joseph. *Youth Knowledge Development Report 2.6; The Labor Market Experience of 14-to-21 Year Olds.* Washington, D.C.: U.S. Department of Labor, Employment and Training Administration, 1980.

Freedman, Marcia. "The Youth Labor Market." In *From School to Work: Improving the Transition.* Prepared for the National Commission for Manpower Policy. Washington, D.C.: U.S. Government Printing Office, 1976.

Friedlander, Stanley L. *Unemployment in the Urban Core: An Analysis of Thirty Cities with Policy Recommendations.* New York: Praeger, 1972.

Gottlieb, David. *Youth and the Meaning of Work.* U.S. Department of Labor, Research and Development Monograph 32. Washington, D.C.: U.S. Government Printing Office, 1973.

National Bureau of Economic Research. *Youth Knowledge Development Report 2.9; The Youth Employment Problem—Dimensions, Causes, and Consequences.* Washington, D.C.: U.S. Department of Labor, Employment and Training Administration, 1980.

National Commission of Employment and Unemployment Statistics. *Counting the Labor Force: Preliminary Report, Prepared for Public Comment.* Washington, D.C.: National Commission of Employment and Unemployment Statistics, 1979.

National Committee on Employment of Youth. *The Transition from School to Work: A Study of Laws, Regulations, and Practices Restricting Work Experience and Employment Opportunities for Youth.* New York: National Committee on Employment of Youth, 1975.

Parnes, Herbert S., and Kohen, Andrew I. "Labor Market Experience of Non-College Youth: A Longitudinal Analysis." In *From School to Work: Improving the Transition.* Prepared for the National Commission for Manpower Policy. Washington, D.C.: U.S. Government Printing Office, 1976.

U.S. Office of Youth Programs. *Youth Knowledge Development Report 2.1: Youth Unemployment—Its Measurement and Meaning.* Washington, D.C.: U.S. Department of Labor, Employment and Training Administration, 1980.

Youth Target Groups; Information and Characteristics:

Barclay, Suzanne; Bottem, Christine; and Fackas, George. *Youth Knowledge Development Report 2.13; Schooling and Work among Youths from Low-Income Households.* Washington, D.C.: U.S. Department of Labor, Employment and Training Administration, 1980.

Klerman, Lorraine, and Jekel, James F. *School-Age Mothers: Problems, Programs, and Policy.* Hamden, Conn.: Shoe String Press, 1973.

Office of Assistant Secretary for Policy, Evaluation, and Research, U.S. Department of Labor. *Youth Knowledge Development Report 2.5; Factbook on Youth.* Washington, D.C.: U.S. Department of Labor, Employment and Training Administration, 1980.

Schorr, Alvin Louis. *Poor Kids.* New York: Basic Books, 1966.

Snedeker, Bonnie. *Youth Knowledge Development Report 2.10; Youth Perspectives—The Lives behind the Statistics.* Prepared for the National Council on Employment Policy, under contract to the U.S. Department of Labor. Washington, D.C.: U.S. Department of Labor, Employment and Training Administration, 1980.

Vocational Foundation, Inc. *Our Turn to Listen: A White Paper on Unemployment, Education, and Crime Based on Extensive Interviews with New York City Dropouts.* New York, n.d.

Wallace, Phyllis Ann. *Pathways to Work: Unemployment among Black Teenage Females.* Lexington, Mass.: Lexington Books, 1974.

Westat, Inc. *Youth Knowledge Development Report 3.10; Characteristics of Enrollees under Age 22 Who Entered CETA Programs during Fiscal Year 1979.* Washington, D.C.: U.S. Department of Labor, Employment and Training Administration, 1980.

Federal Policy and Program Recommendations:

Barton, Paul E. "Youth Transition to Work: The Problem and Federal Policy Setting." In *From School to Work: Improving the Transition.* Prepared for the National Commission for Manpower Policy. Washington, D.C.: U.S. Government Printing Office, 1976.

Briggs, Dennie, and Grant, Douglas. "Developing a Positive National Youth Policy." In *The Value of Youth,* edited by A. Pearl, D. Grant, and E. Wenk. Davis, Calif.: International Dialogue Press, 1978.

Carnegie Council on Policy Studies in Higher Education. *Giving Youth a Better Chance: Options for Education, Work, and Service.* San Francisco: Jossey-Bass, 1979.

Congressional Budget Office. *Budget Options for the Youth Employment Problem.* Washington, D.C.: U.S. Government Printing Office, 1977.

"Feds Plan 1.7 Million Jobs for Youth." *Manpower and Vocational Education Weekly,* 17 May 1979, p. 10.

Levitan, Sar A. "Danger of the Decade: What Shall We Do for (or to) Our Youth?" In *The National CETA Reader* (March 1980): 1.

National Child Labor Committee and National Urban League. *Toward a National Youth Development Policy (A Call to Action).* New York: National Child Labor Committee, 1978.

"No Action Yet on CETA Funding Levels." *Employment and Training Reporter,* 23 December 1981, p. 371.

"OMB Slashes FY 1983 Training Budget." *Employment and Training Reporter,* 9 December 1981, p. 321.

Potomac Institute. *Youth and the Needs of the Nation.* Report of the Committee for the Study of National Service. Washington, D.C.: The Institute, 1979.

"Short-Term Outlook Bleak for Economy and Training Programs, Experts Say." *Employment and Training Reporter,* 23 December 1981, pp. 369-70.

The President. *Economic Report of the President, 1979.* Washington, D.C.: U.S. Government Printing Office, 1979.

The President. *Employment and Training Report of the President, 1978.* Washington, D.C.: U.S. Government Printing Office, 1978.

Taggart, Robert. *Youth Knowledge Development Report 2.12; Youth Employment Policies and Programs for the 1980s—Background Analysis for the Employment and Training Components of the Youth Act of 1980.* Prepared for the Office of Youth Programs. Washington, D.C.: U.S. Department of Labor, Employment and Training Administration, 1980.

Timpane, P. Michael, and others. *Youth Policy in Transition.* Prepared for the Office of the Assistant Secretary for Planning and Evaluation, U.S. Department of Health, Education, and Welfare. Santa Monica, Calif.: The RAND Corporation, 1976.

Public/Private Roles:

American Association of Community and Junior Colleges. *Community and Junior Colleges and the Comprehensive Employment and Training Act: Participation and Recommendations for Improvement.* Washington, D.C.: American Association of Community and Junior Colleges, 1977.

Butler, Eric, and Darr, James. *Youth Knowledge Development Report 2.16; Educator and Employer Perspectives.* Prepared for the Center for Public Service, Brandeis University. Washington, D.C.: U.S. Department of Labor, Employment and Training Administration, 1980.

"Local Officials' Role in Future CETA Slated for Reduction." *Employment and Training Reporter,* 9 December 1981, pp. 313-14.

National Commission for Manpower Policy. *An Enlarged Role for the Private Sector in Federal Employment and Training Programs.* Fourth annual report to the President and the Congress. Washington, D.C.: U.S. Government Printing Office, 1978.

National Governors' Association. *Youth Knowledge Development Report 3.11; The State Role in Youth Employment and Training Programs.* Washington, D.C.: U.S. Department of Labor, Employment and Training Administration, 1980.

"Presidential Task Force on Private Sector Will Promote Volunteerism." *Employment and Training Reporter,* 9 December 1981, pp. 317-18.

Sum, Andrew; Harrington, Paul; and Schneider, Glen. *Youth Knowledge Development Report 3.20; CETA Prime Sponsor Self-Perceptions.* Prepared for the Center for Labor Market Studies, Northeastern University. Washington, D.C.: U.S. Department of Labor, Employment and Training Administration, 1980.

Program Design, Development, and Delivery:

Baltimore. Mayor's Office of Manpower Resources. *Toward a Local Manpower Delivery System: An Annual Report of Services of the Baltimore Metropolitan Manpower Consortium, Fiscal 1977.* Baltimore: MOMR, 1977.

Corporation for Public/Private Ventures. *Youth Knowledge Development Report 8.1; Jobs and Community Improvements—A Handbook for Enhanced Work Projects.* Washington, D.C.: U.S. Department of Labor, Employment and Training Administration, 1980.

Gilsinan, James F., and Tomey, E. Allan. *Youth Knowledge Development Report 7.7; A Comparison of Public and Private Sector Worksites—An In-*

terim Report. Prepared for the Center of Urban Programs, St. Louis University. Washington, D.C.: U.S. Department of Labor, Employment and Training Administration, 1980.

Mangum, Garth L., and Walsh, Jack. *Employment and Training Programs for Youth: What Works Best for Whom?* Report to the Office of Youth Programs, U.S. Employment and Training Administration, from the National Council on Employment Policy. Washington, D.C.: U.S. Employment and Training Administration, 1978.

Manpower Demonstration Research Corporation. *Youth Knowledge Development Report 7.3; Enhanced Work Project—The Supported Work Approach for Youth.* Washington, D.C.: U.S. Department of Labor, Employment and Training Administration, 1980.

National Collaboration for Youth and National Assembly. *Youth Knowledge Development Report 12.1; Linking with Voluntary Youth Serving Agencies.* Washington, D.C.: U.S. Department of Labor, Employment and Training Administration, 1980.

National League of Cities. *Youth Knowledge Development Report 3.18; CETA Youth Programs in Small Cities.* Washington, D.C.: U.S. Department of Labor, Employment and Training Administration, 1980.

National Manpower Institute. *Job Placement Services for Youth.* Washington, D.C.: The Institute, 1978.

Pines, Marion, and Morlock, James. *CETA Program Models: Work Experience Perspectives.* Office of Manpower Research and Development Monograph. Washington, D.C.: U.S. Department of Labor, Employment and Training Administration, 1980.

St. Louis University. *Youth Knowledge Development Report 6.1; Vocational Exploration—Interim Findings and Background.* Washington, D.C.: U.S. Department of Labor, Employment and Training Administration, 1980.

Work in America Institute, Inc. *Job Strategies for Urban Youth: Sixteen Pilot Programs in Action.* Scarsdale, N.Y.: Work in America Institute, 1979.

Program Reviews and Evaluations:

Ball, Joseph, and Diaz, William. *Youth Knowledge Development 11.1; Entitlement Implementation: The First Year's Experience.* Prepared for Manpower Demonstration Research Corporation, under contract to the U.S. Department of Labor. Washington, D.C.: U.S. Department of Labor, Employment and Training Administration, 1980.

Butler, Eric, and Parker, Jim. *Youth Knowledge Development Report 3.19; Lessons from Experience: An Interim Review of the Youth Employment and Demonstrations Projects Act.* Prepared for the Center for Public Service, Brandeis University. Washington, D.C.: U.S. Department of Labor, Employment and Training Administration, 1980.

Clark, Phipps, Clark, and Harris. *Youth Knowledge Development Report 5.3; Advanced Education and Training—Interim Report on the Career Advancement Voucher Demonstration.* Washington, D.C.: U.S. Department of Labor, Employment and Training Administration, 1980.

Corporation for Public/Private Ventures. *Youth Knowledge Development Report*

7.5; Enhanced Work Projects — The Interim Findings from the Ventures in Community Improvement Demonstration. Washington, D.C.: U.S. Department of Labor, Employment and Training Administration, 1980.

Diaz, William; Ball, Joseph; and Jacobs, Nancy. *Youth Knowledge Report 11.2; Entitlement Implementation: Two Years' Experience.* Prepared for Manpower Demonstration Research Corporation, under contract to the U.S. Department of Labor. Washington, D.C.: U.S. Department of Labor, Employment and Training Administration, 1980.

Educational Testing Service. *Youth Knowledge Development Report 6.2; School-to-Work Transition Services — The Initial Findings of the Youth Career Development Program.* Washington, D.C.: U.S. Department of Labor, Employment and Training Administration, 1980.

Goldenberg, I. Ira. *Build Me a Mountain: Youth, Poverty, and the Creation of a New Setting.* Cambridge, Mass.: MIT Press, 1971.

Levitan, Sar A., and Johnston, Benjamin H. *The Job Corps: A Social Experiment that Works.* Baltimore: The Johns Hopkins University Press, 1975.

Mallar, Charles, and Kerachsky, Stuart. *Youth Knowledge Development Report 3.4; The Lasting Impacts of Job Corps Participation.* Prepared for Mathematica Policy Research, Inc. Washington, D.C.: U.S. Department of Labor, Employment and Training Administration, 1980.

National Council on Employment Policy. *CETA's Results and Their Implications.* Washington, D.C.: National Council on Employment Policy, September 1981.

U.S. Office of Youth Programs. *Youth Knowledge Development Report 3.2; Assessments of Job Corps Performance and Impacts.* Vol. 1. Washington, D.C.: U.S. Department of Labor, Employment and Training Administration, 1980.

U.S. Office of Youth Programs. *Youth Knowledge Development Report 3.3; Assessments of Job Corps Performance and Impacts.* Vol. 2. Washington, D.C.: U.S. Department of Labor, Employment and Training Administration, 1980.

U.S. Office of Youth Programs. *Youth Knowledge Development Report 3.8; Youth Initiatives — The Early Experience.* Washington, D.C.: U.S. Department of Labor, Employment and Training Administration, 1980.

U.S. Office of Youth Programs. *Youth Knowledge Development Report 9.1; The Consolidated Youth Employment Program (CYEP) Planning and Early Implementation.* Washington, D.C.: U.S. Department of Labor, Employment and Training Administration, 1980.

Wurzburg, Gregory. *Youth Knowledge Development Report 3.16; Youth and the Local Employment Agenda.* Prepared for the National Council on Employment Policy. Washington, D.C.: U.S. Department of Labor, Employment and Training Administration, 1980.

Research and Evaluation Techniques:

Barton, Paul E., and Fraser, Bryna Shore. *Youth Knowledge Development Report 1.4; A Research and Experimentation Strategy.* Prepared for the National Manpower Institute. Washington, D.C.: U.S. Department of Labor, Employment and Training Administration, 1980.

Bogdan, Robert, and Taylor, Steven J. *Introduction to Qualitative Research*

Methods: A Phenomenological Approach to the Social Sciences. New York: John Wiley and Sons, 1975.

Douglas, Jack D., ed. *Understanding Everyday Life: Toward the Reconstruction of Sociological Knowledge.* Chicago: Aldine Publishing Co., 1970.

Filstead, William J. "Qualitative Methods: A Needed Perspective in Evaluation Research." In *Qualitative and Quantitative Methods in Evaluation Research,* edited by T. Cook and C. Reichart. Beverly Hills: Sage Publications, 1980.

Lofland, John. *Analyzing Social Settings: A Guide to Qualitative Observation and Analysis.* Belmont, Calif.: Wadsworth Publishing Co., 1971.

Stallings, David and McDonnell, Melinda. *Youth Knowledge Development Report 1.5; Evaluation Research in Local Youth Programming.* Prepared for Osoro and Associates, under contract to the U.S. Office of Youth Programs. Washington, D.C.: U.S. Department of Labor, Employment and Training Administration, 1980.

Index

Abortion, 33

Academic ability, 15, 77, 79-81; and GED (General Equivilancy Diploma), 92-93; and grades, 85; and remedial education, 93-94; and school curriculum, 86-87

Addiction, heroin, 57-59

Adolescent parents, 31-36; career outlook, 155-57, 159; employment impediments, 35, 74, 101-2, 138-39; program adjustment difficulties, 114-16, 138-39; school completion, 89; welfare dependency, 32-33, 35-36, 71-74

AFDC (Aid to Families with Dependent Children). See Welfare dependency; Welfare system, inefficiency and inequity of

Alcoholism, 55, 56, 58-61

Appearance, importance of, to youth, 62-63, 77, 82, 114

Athletics: as a career choice, 123, 160-61; in high school, 77, 81

Boston: quality of life in low-income neighborhoods and housing projects of, 49-54; racial prejudice and conflict in, 49-54, 82-84; youth employment and training programs in, 5-10, 52-54, 104-6

Career development: barriers to, 15, 35-36, 37, 54-55, 91, 97-102, 155-60; as a continual and individual process, 15-16, 147-54, 162, 164; versus immediate employment considerations, 98-101, 102-10 passim, 119, 136-37, 147, 149-53, 156, 164

Career exploration: in employment and training programs, 108, 127-32; in high school, 86-88; in military service, 31

Career goals: of youth entering employment and training programs, 15, 102-3, 108-9, 127-30; of youth exiting programs, 147-56

CETA (Comprehensive Employment and Training Act), authorization of youth services under, 3. See also Youth employment and training programs

Communication skills: in family life, 19, 20; in work life, 138-40, 143-44

for youth in, 51, 54-55; youths' views of, 49-55

Conflict with authority: in employment and training programs, 134-36, 139-43; in family life, 23-24, 26-27; in high school, 77-79

Counselors, roles of, in employment and training programs, 41-43, 135-36, 138, 163-64

Delinquency. See Juvenile crime

Discipline and guidance: in high school, 78-79, 81, 86-87; as needs of youth, 20-22, 25-26, 37, 41-43; as a positive factor in career development, 106, 115, 116-17, 135-36, 138-40, 150, 157-58, 162

Dropouts, 88-91

Drugs: alcohol, 55-56, 59-61; heroin and other narcotics, 57-59; marijuana and hashish, 56-57; "psychedelic," 60

Employment: barriers to, for nonmainstream youth, 2-3, 4, 15, 35, 37, 54, 91, 97, 155-59 passim; status of youth, following program participation, 147-60; status of youth, prior to program enrollment, 15, 97-102. See also Work

Family life, 19-46; of adolescent parents, 31-36; contrast between ideal and real, 19-24; economic security, importance in, 20, 43, 46; future plans of youth regarding, 43-46; isolation of youth in, 19-23; in single-parent households, 20-22; successful, factors in, 24-26; without parents, 22; work and, 20, 23-26, 30, 35, 37-40, 43-46, 114-15, 152, 153, 155

GED (General Equivilancy Diploma), 92-95

Grades, in high school, 77, 85. See also Academic ability

High school diploma. See Secondary credential

Individual initiative, importance of, in career development, 39, 44, 109-10, 113-14, 116, 120-21, 125-26, 132, 135, 136-37, 147-

The Johns Hopkins University Press

HARD KNOCKS

This book was composed in Times Roman text by David Lorton, and Windsor Elongated display type by the Composing Room of Baltimore, from a design by Cynthia Hotvedt.
It was printed on Glatfelter's 50-lb. offset paper and bound in Kivar-5 by Thomson-Shore, Inc.